LEARN TO
Sew for the Table

Carefree Picnic Set, page 90

www.companyscoming.com
visit our website

Sushi Time Placemat, page 96

Learn to Sew for the Table

Copyright © Company's Coming Publishing Limited

First Printing November 2009

Library and Archives Canada Cataloguing in Publication
Learn to sew for the table.
(Company's Coming crafts)
Includes index.
ISBN 978-1-897477-25-0
1. Sewing. 2. Tablecloths. 3. Household linens. I. Series: Company's coming crafts
TX879.L43 2009   646.2'1   C2009-901523-4

Published by
Company's Coming Publishing Limited
2311-96 Street
Edmonton, Alberta, Canada T6N 1G3
Tel: 780-450-6223   Fax: 780-450-1857
www.companyscoming.com

Company's Coming is a registered trademark owned by Company's Coming Publishing Limited

Printed in China

The Company's Coming Story

Jean Paré grew up with an understanding that family, friends and home cooking are the key ingredients for a good life. A mother of four, Jean worked as a professional caterer for 18 years, operating out of her home kitchen. During that time, she came to appreciate quick and easy recipes that call for everyday ingredients. In answer to mounting requests for her recipes, Company's Coming cookbooks were born, and Jean moved on to a new chapter in her career.

Company's Coming founder Jean Paré

Just as Company's Coming continues to promote the tradition of home cooking, the same is now true with crafting. Like good cooking, great craft results depend upon easy-to-follow instructions, readily available materials and enticing photographs of the finished products. Also like cooking, crafting is meant to be enjoyed in the home or cottage. Company's Coming Crafts, then, is a natural extension from the kitchen into the family room or den.

In the beginning, Jean worked from a spare bedroom in her home, located in the small prairie town of Vermilion, Alberta, Canada. The first Company's Coming cookbook, *150 Delicious Squares*, was an immediate bestseller. Today, with well over 150 titles in print, Company's Coming has earned the distinction of publishing Canada's most popular cookbooks. The company continues to gain new supporters by adhering to Jean's "Golden Rule of Cooking"—Never share a recipe you wouldn't use yourself. It's an approach that has worked—millions of times over!

Company's Coming cookbooks are distributed throughout Canada, the United States, Australia and other international English-language markets. French and Spanish language editions have also been published. Sales to date have surpassed 25 million copies with no end in sight. Familiar and trusted in home kitchens around the world, Company's Coming cookbooks are highly regarded both as kitchen workbooks and as family heirlooms.

Because Company's Coming operates a test kitchen and not a craft shop, we've partnered with a major North American craft content publisher to assemble a variety of craft compilations exclusively for us. Our editors have been involved every step of the way. You can see the excellent results for yourself in the book you're holding.

Company's Coming Crafts are for everyone—whether you're a beginner or a seasoned pro. What better gift could you offer than something you've made yourself? In these hectic days, people still enjoy crafting parties; they bring family and friends together in the same way a good meal does. Company's Coming is proud to support crafters with this new creative book series.

We hope you enjoy these easy-to-follow, informative and colourful books, and that they inspire your creativity. So, don't delay—get crafty!

TABLE OF CONTENTS

Feeling Crafty? Get Creative! 6 • Foreword 7 • General Instructions 8

Winter

Create a warm and cheery table for celebrating the festive winter holidays with these delightful table sets.

Spring

Set your table for spring with these ensembles that are bursting forth with buds and blooming flowers.

Crazy for Christmas, page 16

Merry Merry Mittens, page 21

Scalloped Table Topper, page 61

Spring in Provence Table Toppings, page 64

TABLE OF CONTENTS

Summer

Stitch up tablecloths, toppers and runners with summertime charm for casual meals both indoors and out.

Autumn

Bring the colours of autumn to your table with ensembles featuring pumpkins, falling leaves and golden sunflowers.

Summer Garden, page 67

Summer Bright Tablecloth, page 76

In the Pumpkin Patch, page 107

Sassy Sunflowers, page 100

Feeling Crafty? Get Creative!

Each 160-page book features easy-to-follow, step-by-step instructions and full-page colour photographs of every project. Whatever your crafting fancy, there's a Company's Coming Creative Series craft book to match!

Beading: Beautiful Accessories in Under an Hour

Complement your wardrobe, give your home extra flair or add an extra-special personal touch to gifts with these quick and easy beading projects. Create any one of these special crafts in an hour or less.

Knitting: Easy Fun for Everyone

Take a couple of needles and some yarn and see what beautiful things you can make! Learn how to make fashionable sweaters, comfy knitted blankets, scarves, bags and other knitted crafts with these easy to intermediate knitting patterns.

Card Making: Handmade Greetings for All Occasions

Making your own cards is a fun, creative and inexpensive way of letting someone know you care. Stamp, emboss, quill or layer designs in a creative and unique card with your own personal message for friends or family.

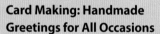

Patchwork Quilting

In this book full of throws, baby quilts, table toppers, wall hangings—and more—you'll find plenty of beautiful projects to try. With the modern fabrics available, and the many practical and decorative applications, patchwork quilting is not just for Grandma!

Crocheting: Easy Blankets, Throws & Wraps

Find projects perfect for decorating your home, for looking great while staying warm or for giving that one-of-a-kind gift. A range of simple but stunning designs make crocheting quick, easy and entertaining.

Sewing: Fun Weekend Projects

Find a wide assortment of easy and attractive projects to help you create practical storage solutions, decorations for any room or just the right gift for that someone special. Create table runners, placemats, baby quilts, pillows and more!

For more information about Company's Coming craft books, visit our website, www.companyscoming.com

FOREWORD

Get ready to sew for your table for every season of the year! In the following pages you'll find many colourful ensembles that will transform an ordinary table into an inviting place to gather. Whether you are dining indoors or outdoors, or planning a gala celebration or an intimate gathering, enhance your table with the perfect coverings to suit any mood.

Start off your holiday celebrations with a whimsical table ensemble using a crazy-patch design or select a fun patchwork runner to light up your table. Add warmth to a winter table with fun print placemats accented with cheery red mittens. For February, choose from several designs to create a romantic table for two or an elegant dinner party for friends.

Set your table for spring with ensembles blooming with flowers. Create a special table for a tea party with delightful placemats, napkins and even a tea cozy featuring yo-yo flowers. Try your hand at sewing a tablecloth for a round or rectangular table, complete with matching napkins.

It may be difficult to decide which sunny summer design you love best! The projects in this chapter include bright and cheery placemats, colourful runners and playful tablecloths. For outdoor dining and picnics, you'll find several fun choices in easy-to-care-for fabrics.

To complete the year, stitch a variety of table projects for autumn featuring falling leaves, pumpkins and golden sunflowers. Easy appliqué designs make stitching a themed table set quick and easy. Your family and friends

will be amazed at your picture-perfect place settings even before the main course is served.

Most of the projects in this book are beginner-level. If you have basic machine-sewing skills, you should be able to complete any of the projects in this book. Creative patterns and a variety of designs make them fun to sew—full-page colour photos and clear, step-by-step instructions with illustrations make it easy. You'll love stitching these fun and fabulous sets for your table all year long!

Bali Tablecloth, page 112

GENERAL INSTRUCTIONS

Basic Sewing Supplies & Equipment

Sewing machine and matching thread

Serger, if desired

Scissors of various sizes, including pinking shears

Rotary cutter(s), mats and straightedges

Pattern-tracing paper or cloth

Pressing tools such as sleeve rolls and
    June Tailor boards

Pressing equipment, including ironing board and iron;
    press cloths

Straight pins and pincushion

Measuring tools

Marking pens (either air- or water-soluble) or
    tailor's chalk

Spray adhesive (temporary)

Hand-sewing needles and thimble

Point turners

How to Appliqué

To ensure success in your appliqué motifs with no wrinkling or puckering, be sure to provide your fabrics with enough stabilizers in the form of interfacing and fusible web. It is best to support both the base fabric and appliqué motif with a nonwoven fusible interfacing; then adhere the motif to the base fabric with fusible web before you begin to stitch.

For pattern templates, using paper and pencil, individually trace each pattern piece onto cardboard or poster board. Cut out each template. These can be used to draw multiple designs.

A pattern frame will help to position the appliqué motifs each time the design is repeated. Transfer the frame outline and the design within the frame onto tracing paper. Cut this out along the frame line.

For each appliqué motif, cut squares of fabric in the appropriate colour and matching size squares of lightweight, fusible interfacing and fusible web. Following the instructions provided by the manufacturers of these products, fuse the interfacing to the wrong side of the fabric; then fuse the web to the interfacing. When the three layers are adhered and have cooled, using the templates, draw the shape needed onto the wrong side of the stabilized fabric. Cut out the appliqué.

To fuse the appliqué, with right side facing up, position motifs as desired on the right side of the base fabric. Using the frame as a guide and looking through its transparency, place it over the fabric motifs and adjust their position. The edge of the frame should surround entire motif appliqués.

On the wrong side of the base fabric, position the interfacing, sticky side down, in alignment with the motif design on the opposite side. *Note: Hold the fabric up to the light to locate the position of the motif.* Fuse the interfacing in place. With interfacing supporting the base and appliqué fabric plus fusible web holding it all in place, you are now free to stitch without fear of puckering.

Set the sewing machine for a zigzag stitch. This will be a medium- to wide-stitch width and a very short stitch length. Attach a zigzag presser foot, and you might consider changing the top tension dial to a buttonhole setting. Practice this satin stitch on a scrap of fabric.

When stitching the motif in place, use a satin stitch and allow the left-hand swing of the needle to catch the motif and the right-hand swing of the needle to enter the base fabric next to the edge of the motif. A medium steady speed is best for satin stitching.

Fusible Tips

When tracing appliqué shapes on the paper side of the fusible web, be sure to allow space between shapes so that each shape is cut loosely around the tracing lines. Cut out each paper shape approximately ¼ inch larger than your drawing lines and iron them onto the wrong side of fabric.

Be sure to follow manufacturer's directions for fusing time, remembering to always test your fusible web on a scrap piece of fabric.

Lay out each appliqué piece before fusing to help you visualize your design. Use a layout that starts at the back and work your way forward. Layering appliqués will give your project depth.

Satin Stitching

Set your sewing machine for a medium to wide zigzag stitch with a very short length.

Attach the zigzag, decorative or satin-stitch presser foot.

Loosen the upper thread tension slightly or to the buttonhole setting indicator.

Using small scraps of fabric, pin a fabric sample to a base-fabric sample to mimic the actual appliqué. Test your stitching on the sample before stitching the appliqué and adjust the stitches as needed. Guide the fabric to allow the right-hand swing of the needle to jump off the appliqué and the left-hand swing to penetrate the appliqué.

Turn the assembly slowly and smoothly on curves to guide the appliqué edge so that it is always held at a 90-degree angle to the stitch width.

For sharp angles, stop the machine with the needle penetrating the fabric, lift the presser foot and rotate the fabric sharply before lowering the foot and continuing to stitch.

Making Bias Strips

Fold fabric on the diagonal (Figure 1) so the lengthwise grain (selvage edge) is parallel to the crosswise grain (cut edge). Pin and press fabric along the fold. Open fold. Measuring from the pressed line, mark points parallel to the pressed line, spacing them the exact cutting width for desired bias width. For the length of each strip, mark a line diagonal to the lengthwise grain of the fabric at each point (Figure 2) to equal the approximate cutting length indicated in the instructions. Cut bias strips.

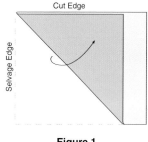

Figure 1

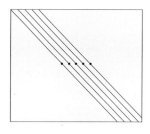

Figure 2

With right sides facing, align the short ends of two strips at right angles (an L shape). Stitch a narrow seam along the diagonal edge. Press the seam open. Continue to join short ends together until you have a continuous loop of bias strips joined together at the short ends in a length equal to the pattern instructions.

Binding Quilt Edges

Join binding strips diagonally and trim seam allowance (Figure 3).

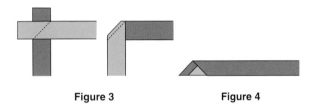

Figure 3   **Figure 4**

Press binding in half with wrong sides together. Unfold one end and trim it at a 45-degree angle; then turn under the edge ½ inch. Refold and press it back again (Figure 4).

With right sides together and raw edges even, sew binding around quilt using a ¼-inch seam allowance, beginning at the centre of one side and stitching until ¼ inch from the first corner. Angle the sewing direction to a 45-degree angle and sew off to the corner point (Figure 5).

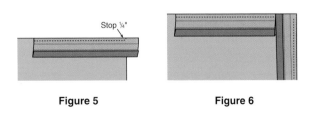

Figure 5   **Figure 6**

Pinch the binding strip in the corner of the quilt, and then reposition the strip along the next side to be stitched. Lay the pinched fabric fold even with the raw edges of the side just stitched (Figure 6). Finish all sides in this manner.

Trim end of binding so it can be tucked inside the pocket at the beginning of the binding, and finish stitching the seam.

Turn the folded edge of the binding over the raw edges and to the back of the quilt. Hand-stitch binding in place.

Mat-Making Basics

If you prefer to make your own placemats, follow these easy steps.

For each placemat, cut two 14 x 19-inch rectangles of fabric. Back one or both with fusible interfacing for more stability.

Embellish the placemat front with appliqués as directed on page 8.

With right sides together and using ½-inch-wide seam allowances, sew the two mats together. Leave a 4-inch-long opening in one long edge and pivot at the beginning and end of the opening as shown in Figure 7.

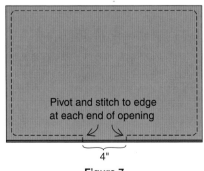

Pivot and stitch to edge
at each end of opening

4"

Figure 7

For smoothly turned corners, stitch to within ½ inch of the corner and then change the stitch length to a short stitch. Continue stitching until you are almost to the pivot point. Pivot and take two stitches across the corner (Figure 8). Pivot, stitch for ½ inch and then return to the normal stitch length until you reach the next corner.

Clip the corners and trim the seams to ¼ inch. Turn the mat right side out and hand-stitch the opening closed.

Topstitch ¼ inch from the outer edges if desired.

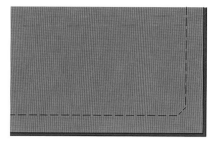

Figure 8

Fabric Yardage

Tablecloth Yardage

		Fabric Width	
Table Diameter	Tablecloth Diameter	36–45 inches	54 inches
34–38 inches	50 inches	3 yards	1½ yards
39–43 inches	55 inches	3¼ yards	1⅝ yards
44–48 inches	60 inches	3½ yards	1¾ yards
49–53 inches	65 inches	3¾ yards	1⅞ yards
54–58 inches	70 inches	4 yards	2 yards

Tablecloth Scallops

Table Diameter	Cloth Diameter per quarter	No. of Scallops Around ¼ Circumference	Scallop Diameter
34–38 inches	50 inches	8	4⅞ inches
39–43 inches	55 inches	8	5¼ inches
44–48 inches	60 inches	8	5⅜ inches
49–53 inches	65 inches	10	5⅛ inches
54–58 inches	70 inches	10	5½ inches

HOLIDAY LIGHTS TABLE RUNNER

Light up your holiday table with this inspirational quilted table runner.

Design | Carolyn Vagts

Skill Level
Easy

Finished Size
24½ x 52½ inches

Materials
44/45-inch-wide cotton fabric:
⅜ yard cream
3 yards dark green
⅙ yard each 4 green prints
Scraps bright-colour batiks and gold fabric for lightbulb appliqués
Gold embroidery thread for light cord
¼ yard fusible web
26 x 50 inches needlepunched insulated batting

Cutting
From cream fabric:
• Cut one 12½ x 40½-inch rectangle for runner centre.

From dark green fabric:
• Cut three 1¼-inch strips the width of the fabric. Subcut into two 40½-inch lengths and two 12½-inch lengths for flange strips.

• Cut two 4½ x 44½-inch strips for long outer borders and two 4½ x 16½-inch strips for short outer borders.

• Cut four 2½-inch strips the width of the fabric for binding.

From each of the four green prints:
• Cut one 2½-inch strip the width of the fabric for inner border and corner blocks.

From scraps of bright-colour batik and gold fabric:
• Using template provided (see page 15), enlarge 200 per cent and trace lightbulbs onto paper side of fusible web for lightbulb appliqués. Cut out just outside traced lines. Fuse onto fabrics; cut out on traced lines. *Note: Model project uses four lightbulbs across each end of runner and six across each side.*

Assembly
Use ¼-inch seam allowances unless otherwise indicated. Sew right sides together.

Sew together one each of the four strips for inner border along long edges to make a piece 8½ inches by the width of the fabric (Figure 1).

Figure 1

Holiday Lights Table Runner

From pieced unit, cut 14 (2½ x 8½-inch) sections (Figure 2). Reserve the rest for corner squares.

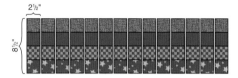

Figure 2

For inner borders, sew five of the 2½ x 8½-inch sections together to make a 40½-inch-long strip, and two units to make a 16½-inch-long strip (Figure 3). Repeat to make another 40½-inch strip and 16½-inch strip.

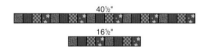

Figure 3

Fold and press flange strips in half with wrong sides together. With raw edges even, sew with a scant ¼-inch seam to each long edge of centre fabric and then to short edges (Figure 4).

Figure 4

Referring to Figure 5, sew inner border strips to top, bottom and to sides of centre unit. Press.

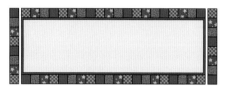

Figure 5

Sew long outer border strips to long edges of runner unit (Figure 6).

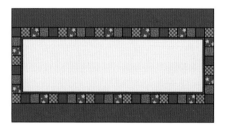

Figure 6

From leftover pieced unit, cut four 2½ x 8½-inch strips. Pull the stitching out of the centre seam in each strip to make each unit 2½ x 4½ inches. Sew units together to make four Four-Patch units (Figure 7). Press.

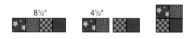

Figure 7

Sew one Four-Patch unit to the end of each short outer border strip. Sew short outer border strips to ends of unit (Figure 8).

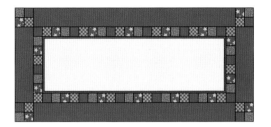

Figure 8

Fuse lightbulb appliqués into place around border. Transfer light cord or draw freehand using air-soluble marker. Satin-stitch cord using gold embroidery thread.

Cut backing from dark green fabric. Sandwich batting between backing and completed top, and pin or baste in place. Straight-stitch around edges of appliqués using matching thread in needle and dark green in bobbin. Quilt as desired.

Refer to General Instructions to bind quilt edges (see page 10). ■

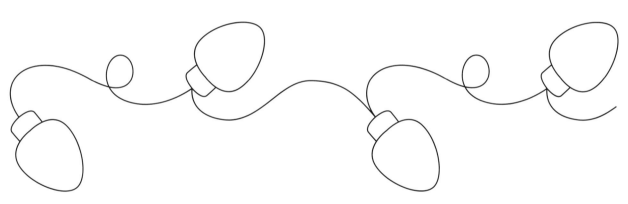

Holiday Lights Table Runner
Lightbulb Template
Enlarge 200%

CRAZY FOR CHRISTMAS

Tuck flatware into crazy patchwork stockings that can double as ornaments, and then set the table with colourful matching placemats.

Designs | Janis Bullis

Skill Level
Easy

Finished Sizes
Placemat: 12 x 18 inches
Stocking: 5 x 10 inches

Materials for One Three-Piece Place Setting
44/45-inch-wide washable linen or linen/
    cotton-blend fabric:
        ⅝ yard gold
        ½ yard each red and green
        ¼ yard each royal blue and purple
¼ yard each 5 different narrow decorative ribbons
All-purpose thread to match fabrics and ribbons
3 yards filler cord for matching piping or 3 yards
    purchased piping in a colour that matches or
    coordinates with the fabric colour(s)
Pattern-tracing cloth
14 x 20-inch rectangle lightweight quilt batting
⅜ yard red cotton for stocking lining
¼ yard ⅝-inch-wide red grosgrain ribbon for
    hanging loop
Temporary spray adhesive
Several small coordinating buttons and/or other
    embellishments
Zipper foot
Point presser

Cutting
Enlarge patterns for stocking, placemat centre and placemat border as directed on pages 19 & 20. Use the patterns to cut the required pieces as directed.

From red linen:
• Cut one stocking back and one placemat border.

• Cut one 13 x 19-inch rectangle for the placemat back. Set the remaining fabric aside for the patchwork.

From green linen:
• Cut four 1⅛ x 26-inch true-bias strips for the piping. Set the scraps aside for the patchwork.

From red cotton:
• Cut two stockings for the stocking lining.

Crazy Patchwork Assembly
Note: *Use ¼-inch-wide seams.*

Begin by cutting each colour fabric in roughly 4–6-inch shapes with odd angles (Figure 1).

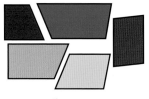

Figure 1

Crazy for Christmas

Combining colours at random and using ¼-inch-wide seam allowances, stitch pieces together in pairs. Press the seam allowance open in each pair. Stitch two pairs or single pieces together with seams perpendicular to each other (Figure 2).

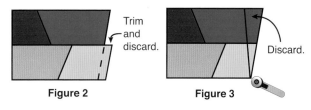

Figure 2   **Figure 3**

Mark and trim on the edge of the resulting piece at a new angle (Figure 3).

Add a third pair (Figure 4). Continue to add fabric pieces, working from the centre out to create a 14 x 20-inch piece of patchwork for the placemat centre and a 7 x 11-inch piece for the stocking. As the piece for the placemat centre grows, you may need to join two pairs before adding them to the centre. Anything goes with crazy piecing.

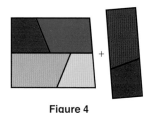

Figure 4

Stitch decorative ribbons along some of the seam lines as desired to embellish the patchwork.

Placemat Assembly

Note: *Use ½-inch-wide seam allowances.*

Staystitch the placemat border ⅜ inch from the inner raw edge. Fold the border in quarters to locate the centres and mark them with a ⅛-inch-long snip. Clip the inner rounded corners to the staystitching in ¼- or ½-inch increments (Figure 5).

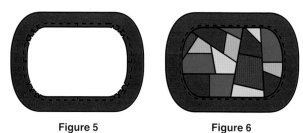

Figure 5   **Figure 6**

Fold the patchwork rectangle in half and then in half again and use the pattern for the placemat centre to cut out the patchwork centre. Before unfolding, make ⅛-inch-long snips to mark the centres.

With right sides facing and centre snips matching all around, pin and stitch the border to the patchwork centre. Press the seam toward the border. Topstitch close to the border edge through all layers (Figure 6).

Use the completed front as a pattern to trim the placemat back and batting rectangles to match. Apply a light coat of temporary spray adhesive to the wrong side of the placemat front and smooth in place on the batting. Machine-baste ¼ inch from the outer edge.

Sew the 1⅛ x 26-inch bias strips together with bias seams to make one long strip; press the seams open. Wrap the strip around the cord with wrong sides together and raw edges even. Attach the zipper foot and adjust it to the

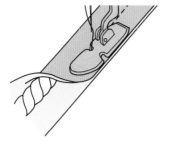

Figure 7

right of the needle. Stitch close to the cord to complete enough piping for the placemat and the stocking (Figure 7).

Thread the machine with a contrasting thread colour in the bobbin and adjust the machine for a basting-length stitch. With raw edges even, pin and machine-baste the piping to the right side of the placemat. To turn the curves, clip the piping seam

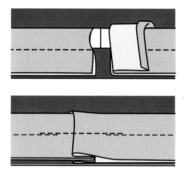

Figure 8
Join piping ends.

allowance as needed. Leave a few inches of overlap where the piping ends meet. Neatly join the piping end to the beginning as shown in Figure 8.

With right sides facing, pin the placemat back to the placemat front. With the back of the placemat front facing you, stitch just inside the basting stitching, leaving a 6-inch-long opening at one long edge for turning.

Turn the placemat right side out and turn in the opening edges. Slipstitch the edges together along the stitching line on the back of the placemat. Press.

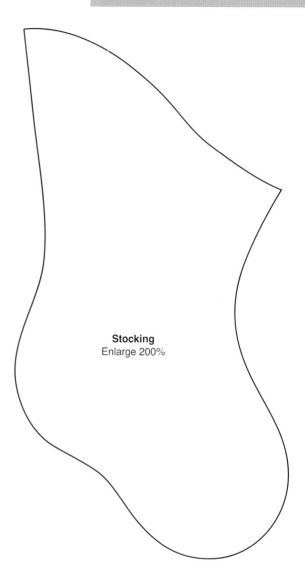

Stocking
Enlarge 200%

Stocking Assembly

Use the stocking pattern to cut one stocking from the patchwork. Apply piping to the outer edge as described for the placemat, beginning and ending at the upper edge.

With right sides facing, pin the stocking front to the stocking back. Stitch just inside the basting. Trim the seam allowance to ¼ inch and turn right side out.

With raw edges even, pin and machine-baste the remaining piping to the patchwork stocking upper edge. Join piping ends at the centre back as described for the placemat and shown in Figure 8, see page 19.

Fold the ribbon in half to make the hanging loop and baste in place at the upper edge on the stocking back, close to the back seam.

With right sides facing, pin and stitch the stocking lining pieces together. Leave a 4-inch-long opening in the back seam for turning. Trim the seam allowance to ¼ inch. Do not turn the lining right side out.

Tuck the stocking into the lining with right sides facing and upper raw edges aligned. Stitch just inside the basting around the upper edge. Turn the stocking right side out through the opening in the lining. Turn in and press the opening edges and topstitch the folded edges together. Tuck the completed lining inside the stocking. ■

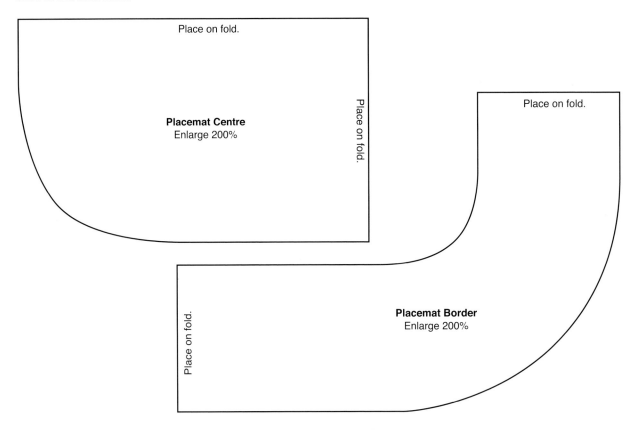

Place on fold.

Placemat Centre
Enlarge 200%

Place on fold.

Place on fold.

Place on fold.

Placemat Border
Enlarge 200%

MERRY MERRY MITTENS

Set a cheery table with this table runner and matching placemats. Red mittens and wintry prints add up to a colourful backdrop for winter entertaining.

Designs | Michelle Crawford

Skill Level
Easy

Finished Sizes
Placemat: 12½ x 18½ inches
Napkins: 18½ x 18½ inches
Table Runner: 14½ x 28½ inches

Materials for Runner & Two Place Settings
44/45-inch-wide cotton prints:
  1 yard snowman print for outer borders and napkins
  1½ yards snowflake print for placemat borders and backing for runner and mats
  ⅝ yard blue print (with stripes) for the sashing and binding
  ⅛ yard red tone-on-tone print for hearts and mittens
  ¼ yard white tone-on-tone print for blocks
2 (14 x 21-inch) pieces cotton batting for placemats
1 (16 x 30-inch) piece cotton batting for table runner
Paper-backed fusible web
Machine quilting thread in matching colours
Pencil
Rotary cutter, mat and ruler

Cutting
From the snowman print:
• Cut three 3½ x 40-inch strips. From these strips, cut two 3½ x 8½-inch strips, four 3½ x 12½-inch strips and two 3½ x 22½-inch strips.

• Cut two 19½-inch squares for the napkins.

From the snowflake print:
• Cut two 14 x 21-inch placemat backing rectangles and one 16 x 30-inch runner backing rectangle.

• Cut two 2½ x 40-inch strips; crosscut four 2½ x 8½-inch strips and four 2½ x 12½-inch strips for the placemats.

From the blue print (with stripes):
• Cut six 2¼ x 40-inch binding strips.

• Cut four 1½ x 40-inch strips; crosscut eight 1½ x 6½-inch sashing strips, four 1½ x 8½-inch sashing strips and two 1½ x 22½-inch sashing strips.

From the white tone-on-tone print:

• Cut one 6½ x 40-inch strip. Crosscut into five 6½-inch squares for the mitten blocks.

• From the remainder of the strip, cut four 3½-inch corner squares for runner.

Note: You will cut the appliqués from the red print later.

Assembly

Use ¼-inch-wide seam allowance unless otherwise indicated.

Referring to Figure 1, arrange the pieces for each placemat. Sew the 6½-inch-long striped sashing strips to opposite sides of the centre square and press the seams away from the centre square. Add the 8½-inch-long sashing strips to the remaining raw edges and press the seams away from the centre square. Sew the 8½-inch snowflake border strips to the top and bottom edges and press the seams toward the borders.

Sew the inner and outer side border strips together and press the seams toward the outer borders. Add the border units to the placemat and press the seams toward the outer border. Set the placemat panels aside.

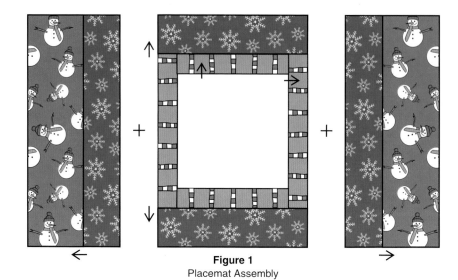

Figure 1
Placemat Assembly

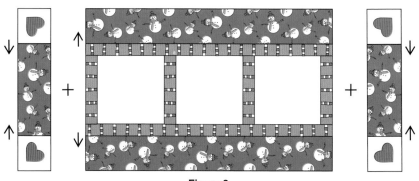

Figure 2
Runner Assembly

Referring to Figure 2, arrange and sew the blocks and 1½ x 6½-inch sashing strips together. Press the seams toward the sashing strips. Add the long sashing strips to the top and bottom edges of the panel and press the seams toward the sashing strips. Add the 3½ x 22½-inch outer border strips and press the seams toward the borders.

Merry Merry Mittens

Sew white corner squares to opposite ends of the 3½ x 8½-inch outer border strips and press the seams toward the borders. Sew the border strips to the centre panel and press the seams toward the borders.

For each placemat, smooth a 14 x 21-inch piece of batting on the wrong side of a 14 x 21-inch backing rectangle. Centre a placemat faceup on top and pin or hand-baste the layers together. Layer the table runner with batting and backing in the same manner.

Using white quilting thread, stitch in the ditch around each white square. Change to light blue quilting thread; stitch in the ditch of all remaining seams to quilt the layers together in each placemat and the table runner. Stipple-quilt the outer borders of the table runner or use a quilting design of your choice.

Machine-stitch ⅛ inch from the outer edges of the placemats and the runner. Trim the excess batting and backing even with the placemat and runner edges.

Sew the binding strips together to make one long strip. Press the seams open. Fold the strip in half lengthwise with raw edges even and wrong sides together. Press. Turn under one end at a 45-degree angle and press. Trim the excess (Figure 3).

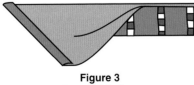

Figure 3
Prepare binding.

Beginning with the turned end of the binding, somewhere past the centre of the lower raw edge of the runner, pin and sew the binding in place. Mitre each corner as you reach it. Where the ends meet, overlap the turned end and trim the excess binding. Sew binding to each placemat in the same manner.

Turn the binding over the raw edges to the wrong side, mitre the corners and slipstitch the folded edges to the backing of each piece.

Trace four hearts, five right mittens and five left mittens onto the paper side of the fusible web. Cut out each piece with at least a ¼-inch margin all around. Apply the fusible web pieces to the wrong side of the red tone-on-tone print following the manufacturer's directions. Cut out on the drawn lines and remove the paper backing.

Referring to the photo (see page 23), arrange two mittens on each 6½-inch white block and fuse in place following the manufacturer's directions. Position the hearts in the corner blocks of the runner and fuse in place.

Use a pencil to draw a line to connect the mittens on each block.

With dark blue quilting thread, satin-stitch over the pencil lines. Change to an appliqué stitch if available on your machine, and stitch around the outer edges of the mittens and the hearts. Satin-stitch these edges if you prefer.

Finish each napkin square with a narrow double hem. Topstitch with white thread. ■

**Templates for
Merry Merry Mittens**
Actual Size

ROMANTIC TABLE SETTING

Sheer fabrics set the mood for romance with this special table setting. Embellished with delicate heart rosettes, it's perfect for Valentine's Day, bridal parties or anniversary celebrations.

Designs | Kenna Prior

Skill Level
Intermediate

Finished Sizes
Tablecloth: 68 x 83 inches, excluding trim
Chair Cover: 13¼ x 37¼, excluding trim

Materials for Tablecloth, Four Chair Covers & Four Napkin Rings
44/45-inch-wide fabric:
  5½ yards lightweight polyester
  3 yards coordinating sheer polyester
Polyester sewing thread to match fabrics
3 yards white 2-inch-wide wire-edge sheer ribbon
6 yards pearl beaded trim
8 white small hook-and-loop circles
Hand-sewing needle
Sewing machine with zigzag stitch

Tablecloth

Cutting
From lightweight polyester fabric:
• Cut one 45 x 60-inch piece for tablecloth centre.

• Cut four 13 x 13-inch squares for bottom layer of corner panels.

• Cut two 7 x 60-inch pieces for side border B.

• Cut two 7 x 45-inch pieces for end border D.

From sheer polyester fabric:
• Cut four 13 x 13-inch squares for top layer of corner panels.

• Cut two 7 x 60-inch pieces for side border A.

• Cut two 7 x 45-inch pieces for end border E.

Assembly
Serge or straight-stitch all seams using ⅜-inch allowance. Finish raw edges of straight-stitch seams with overcast or zigzag. Stitch all pieces right sides together unless otherwise stated.

Stitch one side border A piece and one side border B piece together. Repeat with remaining side border pieces. Stitch each assembled side border to matching side edges of tablecloth centre piece according to Assembly Diagram on page 32.

Stitch one end border D piece and one end border E piece together. Repeat with remaining end border pieces.

For each corner panel, place one sheer 13 x 13-inch square over right side of one lightweight 13 x 13-inch square. Stitch around outer edge.

Romantic Table Setting

Stitch one corner panel to each end of each assembled end border. Stitch each assembled end border to tablecloth centre and side borders. Trim off excess raw edge of each side border.

Cut beaded trim to fit across edges of each corner panel. Working at one corner at a time, turn raw edge under ⅜ inch and match header on trim to fold on right side of fabric. Stitch across edges. When this edge is folded under again as you hem remainder of tablecloth, the fringe will hang down from the underside of the tablecloth.

Stitch a ⅜-inch double-fold hem around outer edge of assembled tablecloth. Sew one heart rosette (instructions follow) to each corner panel (see photo page 27).

Chair Cover

Cutting
Instructions are for a single chair cover.

From lightweight polyester fabric:
• Cut one 14 x 32-inch piece.

• Cut one 13 x 13-inch square.

From sheer polyester fabric:
• Cut one 13 x 13-inch square.

Assembly
Serge or straight-stitch all seams using ⅜-inch allowance. Finish raw edges of straight-stitch seams with overcast or zigzag. Stitch all pieces right sides together unless otherwise stated.

For insert, place one sheer 13 x 13-inch square over right side of one lightweight 13 x 13-inch square. Stitch around outer edge.

On one short edge of 14 x 32-inch piece, cut a 12-inch slit at centre of edge.

Match two edges of insert with edges of 12-inch slit. Stitch along edges. Clip seam at V-point of inset.

Assembly Diagram

Attach beaded fringe and hem assembled cover same as for tablecloth.

Sew loop sides of two hook-and-loop circles to corners of straight end on wrong side of cover. Lining them up with the V-point of cover, sew hook side of circles on right side of cover at each edge.

Attach rosette (instructions follow) to cover over V-point of inset.

Heart Rosette

Note: You will need four rosettes for the tablecloth, one for each chair cover and one for each napkin ring.

Cutting

From sheer polyester fabric:
• Cut one 3 x 18-inch piece.

From ribbon:
• Cut one 8-inch length.

From beaded trim.
• Cut one piece with four strands.

Assembly

Fold 8-inch ribbon in half. Twist ends of wire together on one edge. Gather opposite edge to measure about 1 inch (photo 2a) and twist ends of wire together. Fold ends of ribbon in half and twist wires together (photo 2b). Shape 1-inch edge into a closed oval on front of piece and shape other edge to form a heart (photo 2c).

 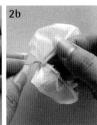 

Fold sheer strip in half lengthwise, wrong sides together. Turn the short edges to inside about ¼ inch and pin in place. Run a gathering thread across long raw edges of the folded piece. Pull thread tightly to form a ruffled rosette. Secure gathering thread.

Roll up the header on the beaded trim piece to fit the centre back of the rosette and tack in place using the remainder of gathering thread. Run the thread back through centre to front of rosette. Thread on a large bead cut from trim and run through centre to back. Tack rosette over centre opening on front of the ribbon heart.

Napkin Ring

Cutting

Instructions are for a single napkin ring.

From lightweight polyester:
• Cut one 5 x 6-inch piece.

Assembly

Serge or straight-stitch all seams using ⅜-inch allowance. Finish raw edges of straight-stitch seams with overcast or zigzag. Stitch all pieces right sides together unless otherwise stated.

Fold piece in half matching 6-inch edges. Stitch raw edges together. Flatten piece with seam at centre back of piece. Press seam open. Turn.

Match short edges of piece with seam line out. Stitch edges together. Turn.

Sew one rosette to ring with seam centred at back. ∎

LOVE IS IN THE STARS!

Combine easy appliqué and piecing with cheery prints to create this lighthearted table setting. It's perfect for a valentine luncheon—or just because.

Designs | Michele Crawford

Skill Level
Easy

Finished Sizes
Placemat: 12½ x 18½ inches
Napkin: 19 x 19 inches
Table Runner: 12½ x 42½ inches

Materials for Runner & Two Place Settings
44/45-inch-wide cotton fabrics:
⅓ yard pink/blue plaid for star points
⅝ yard white tone-on-tone print for block centres, edges and corners
⅝ yard blue floral print for sashing and borders
1⅜ yards pink print for napkins, heart appliqués and binding
1⅜ yards multicoloured plaid or bold check for placemat borders, placemat backing and runner backing
1 yard low-loft batting
¼ yard paper-backed fusible web
Note: Preshrink fabrics before cutting. Usable fabric width should be 40 inches after washing.

Cutting
From white tone-on-tone print for block background:
• Cut six 4½-inch squares for the block centres.

• Cut three 2½ x 40-inch strips; subcut strips into 24 (2½ x 4½-inch) rectangles for block edges.

• Cut two 2½ x 40-inch strips; subcut strips into 24 (2½-inch) squares for corners.

From pink/blue plaid for star points:
• Cut three 2½ x 40-inch strips; subcut strips into 48 (2½-inch) squares.

From blue floral print for sashing and borders:
• Cut seven 2½ x 40-inch strips. Set aside three of these strips for runner borders.

• From the remaining strips, cut nine 2½ x 8½-inch strips and four 2½ x 12½-inch strips.

From pink print for napkins, binding and heart appliqués:
• Cut two 24-inch squares for the napkins.

• Cut six 2¼ x 40-inch strips for binding strips.

• Cut one 4½ x 40-inch strip. Apply fusible web. Using pattern provided (see page 31), cut out six heart appliqués.

From multicoloured plaid or bold check for runner backing, placemat backing and placemat borders:
• Cut one 13 x 43-inch strip from the length of the fabric for the runner backing.

• Cut two 13 x 19-inch pieces for placemat backing.

• Cut four 3½ x 12½-inch strips for placemat borders.

From batting:
• Cut two 13 x 19-inch pieces for placemats.

• Cut one 13 x 43-inch strip for runner.

Block Assembly

Use ¼-inch-wide seam allowances throughout.

With right sides together and raw edges aligned, stitch a 2½-inch pink/blue plaid square to each end of each 2½ x 4½-inch white rectangle (Figure 1). Trim away the corner ¼ inch from the stitching. Press the triangle toward the seam allowance to make 24 star-point units.

Sew two star-point units to opposite sides of a centre block. Sew a white corner block to each end of two star-point units (Figure 2). Press seams in direction of arrows. Sew units together to make a block. Repeat to make six blocks.

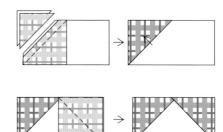

Figure 1

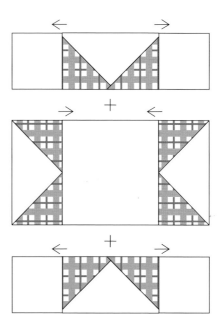

Figure 2

Placemat & Napkin Assembly

Note: Repeat placemat instructions to make two placemats.

Sew a 2½ x 8½-inch blue floral print strip to the top and bottom of one block. Press the seams toward the strips.

Arrange two 2½ x 12½-inch blue floral strips and two 3½ x 12½-inch placemat multicoloured border strips as shown in Figure 3. Sew together for placemat top. Press all seams away from the centre blocks.

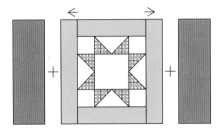

Figure 3

For each placemat, pin batting between the wrong sides of a 13 x 19-inch backing piece and a pieced placemat top. Use white machine-quilting thread to stitch in the ditch around the outer edges of each centre square. Stitch in the ditch of the vertical border seams. Stitch the layers together ⅛ inch from the outer edge of the placemat; trim the batting and backing even with the pieced placemat edges.

Using bias seams, sew the 2¼-inch-wide pink print binding strips together to make one long strip; press the seams open (Figure 4). Fold the strip in half lengthwise with wrong sides together and press. Bind edges of each placemat with the bias strip, mitering corners and overlapping ends to finish. *Note: Remaining bias strip will be used on the runner.*

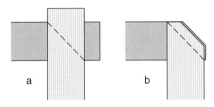

a   b

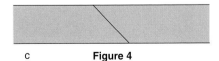

c   **Figure 4**

Remove the paper backing from two heart appliqués. Position and fuse a heart in the centre of the star block on each placemat. Appliqué (blanket-stitch or pin-stitch) around the outer edge of each heart.

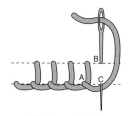

Blanket Stitch

Turn under, press and sew a narrow double hem on each napkin square.

Runner Assembly
Note: Refer to Figure 5 throughout Runner Assembly.

Sew remaining four blocks and five 2½ x 8½-inch blue floral print sashing strips together for runner (Figure 5). Press all seams toward blue strips.

Sew the three remaining 2½ x 40-inch blue floral print strips together using bias seams. Press the seams open. From the strip, cut two 2½ x 42½-inch border strips. Sew these strips to opposite edges of the panel to complete the pieced runner top (Figure 5).

Figure 5

Pin runner batting between 13 x 43-inch runner backing and pieced runner top. Stitch in the ditch around the outer edges of each centre square. Stitch in the ditch of the vertical border seams. Stipple-quilt the sashing and border strips with blue machine-quilting thread. Stitch ⅛ inch from the outer edges of the pieced runner. Trim batting and backing even with the edges of top.

Remove the paper backing from four heart appliqués. Position and fuse a heart in the centre of each star block on runner. Appliqué (blanket-stitch or pin-stitch) around the outer edge of each heart. ■

Love Is in the Stars!
Appliqué Template
Actual Size

SEW A WINE & DINE PICNIC

Set up your next picnic in front of a roaring fire after you create this pretty six-piece set to chase away winter blues.

Designs | June McCrary Jacobs

Skill Level
Easy

Finished Sizes
Napkin: 14½ x 14½ inches
Wine Glass Bag: 5 x 10 inches
Wine Bottle Bag: 5¼ x 18¼ inches, excluding handle
Flatware Carrier: 15½ x 12½ inches, unfolded
Basket Liner: 21½ x 27¾ inches
Blanket/Tablecloth: 43 x 51½ inches

Materials
44/45-inch-wide fabric:
    1 yard red polished cotton
    2 yards small-check red-and-white gingham
    1 yard floral print blue denim
    1 yard white solid broadcloth
    ¾ yard denim-blue broadcloth
    2½ yards patterned blue-and-white broadcloth
1 yard medium-weight interfacing
45 x 60-inch needled cotton batting
3¼ yds red grosgrain ribbon
3 (3-yard) packages red double-fold bias quilt binding
Large oblong basket with handles
Optional: 2 strawberry floral picks
Note: Materials listed are sufficient to make one each wine bottle bag, flatware carrier, basket liner and blanket/tablecloth, and two each napkins and wine glass bags.

Cutting
From red polished cotton:
• Cut two 15½ x 15½-inch squares for reversible napkins.

• Use pattern on page 45 to cut 4 large hearts for appliqué onto blanket/tablecloth.

• Use pattern on page 45 to cut two small hearts for lining for gingham appliqués on reversible napkins.

From red-and-white gingham:
• Cut two 20 x 15½-inch rectangles for flatware carrier.

• Cut two 15½ x 15½-inch squares for reversible napkins.

• Cut eight 11 x 7-inch rectangles for wine glass bags.

• Cut four 19 x 7½-inch rectangles for wine bottle bag.

• Use pattern on page 45 to cut two small hearts for appliqué on reversible napkins.

From floral print blue denim:
• Cut two 28 x 22-inch rectangles for basket liner.

From white solid broadcloth:
• Cut four 9 x 10-inch rectangles for blanket/tablecloth.

• Use pattern on page 45 to cut four large hearts for lining for red heart appliqués on blanket/tablecloth.

From denim-blue broadcloth:
• Cut two 28 x 10-inch rectangles for blanket/tablecloth.

From patterned blue-and-white broadcloth:
• Cut one 44 x 35-inch rectangle for blanket/tablecloth front.

• Cut one 44 x 53-inch rectangle for blanket/tablecloth backing.

From batting:
• Cut one 20 x 15½-inch rectangle for flatware carrier.

• Cut two 19 x 7½-inch rectangles for wine bottle bag.

• Cut four 11 x 7-inch rectangles for wine glass bags.

• Cut one 28 x 22-inch rectangle for denim basket liner.

From medium-weight interfacing:
• Cut four 9 x 10-inch rectangles for blanket/tablecloth.

From grosgrain ribbon:
• Cut two 26-inch lengths for wine glass bags.

• Cut one 20-inch length for wine bottle bag.

• Cut one 40-inch length for flatware carrier.

Wine Glass Bag Assembly

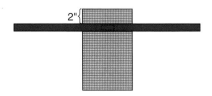

Layer each 11 x 7-inch rectangle of batting between two 11 x 7-inch gingham rectangles to make four layered sets. Machine-baste ¼ inch around edges of each set.

Centre one 26-inch length of grosgrain ribbon 2 inches from top edge of one set (Figure 1). Stitch in place to make one bag back. Repeat to make a second bag back. Remaining two sets will be bag fronts.

Figure 1

With ribbon on outside, match bag fronts and backs. Sew sides and bottoms together a scant ¼ inch from edges. Trim stray threads and corners; turn and press.

Making sure ribbon ends are not within seam allowance, sew sides and bottom again using a ⅝-inch seam allowance, enclosing the previous seams. Turn right side out; press.

Bind raw top edge with double-fold bias quilt binding.

Sew a Wine & Dine Picnic

Wine Bottle Bag Assembly

Layer 19 x 7½-inch rectangles of batting between 19 x 7½-inch gingham rectangles for bag front and back. Baste ¼ inch from edges.

Centre one 20-inch length of grosgrain ribbon 4 inches from top edge of bag back (Figure 2). Stitch in place.

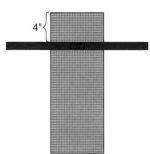
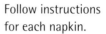

Figure 2

Finish as in Wine Glass Bag Assembly. Cut a 10-inch length of double-fold bias quilt binding. Press under ends and stitch; sew edges of binding together. Sew ends inside top of bag at side seams for handle.

Reversible Napkin Assembly

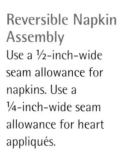

Use a ½-inch-wide seam allowance for napkins. Use a ¼-inch-wide seam allowance for heart appliqués.

Follow instructions for each napkin.

Sew one small red heart and one small gingham heart with right sides together. Clip corners, points and curves. Carefully separate layers and snip a 1-inch horizontal opening in the centre of the red heart. Turn hearts right side out through opening. Press.

Fold red 15½ x 15½-inch square in fourths. Centre heart appliqué on one quarter with point of heart approximately 3 inches from corner point. Pin appliqué in place. Stitch heart to red square using zigzag stitch and red thread.

Sew one 15½ x 15½-inch red square and one 15½ x 15½-inch gingham square together, leaving an opening for turning.

Trim corners and turn right side out. Press. Using white thread, zigzag-stitch around napkin edges. Zigzag ¼ inch around heart appliqué.

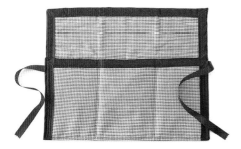

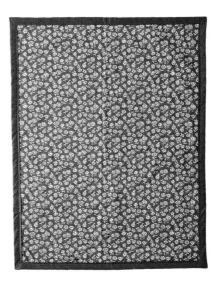

Flatware Carrier Assembly

Layer 20 x 15½-inch rectangle of batting between 20 x 15½-inch rectangles of gingham. Baste ¼ inch from edges. Press.

Bind all four raw edges with double-fold bias quilt binding, mitring corners.

Centre 40-inch length of ribbon 6 inches from top on one side; sew in place.

With ribbon side on bottom, fold bottom edge of rectangle up 7½ inches. Stitch as shown in Figure 3 to form pockets.

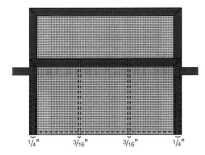

1/4"   3/16"   3/16"   1/4"

Figure 3

Basket Liner Assembly

Layer 28 x 22-inch rectangle of batting between 28 x 22-inch rectangles of floral print blue denim fabric. Baste ¼ inch from edges.

Bind edges with double-fold bias quilt binding, mitring corners.

Blanket/Tablecloth Assembly

Use ½-inch-wide seam allowances unless otherwise indicated.

Sew one large red heart and one large heart white lining with right sides together. Clip corners, points and curves. Carefully separate layers and snip a 1-inch horizontal opening in the centre of the white heart. Turn hearts right side out through opening. Press. Repeat to make four hearts.

Place each heart on a 9 x 10-inch white rectangle, centred side to side and 3½ inches from one corner. Refer to Assembly Diagram for placement. *Note: The top of the rectangle will be one of the 9-inch edges.*

Using white thread, straight-stitch around hearts close to finished edges. Stitch again around hearts ¼ inch inside previous stitching using white thread and zigzag stitch.

With red thread, zigzag around hearts ¼ inch outside finished edges.

Referring to the Assembly Diagram, sew inside edge of each heart block to 10-inch edges of denim blue rectangles. Press seams toward blue rectangles.

For front, sew heart/denim-blue units to 35-inch edges of patterned blue-and-white broadcloth rectangle. Press seams toward denim-blue rectangles. Topstitch ⅜ inch from sewing line on all seams using a long straight stitch with white thread.

Sew front and 44 x 53-inch patterned blue-and-white broadcloth with right sides together, leaving an opening for turning.

Trim corners. Turn right side out and press. Slipstitch opening closed. Topstitch ⅜ inch from edge. ∎

Blanket/Tablecloth Assembly Diagram

Large Heart

Small Heart

Sew a Wine & Dine Picnic Templates
Actual Size

Spring's in the Basket

Pretty beribboned baskets in saturated pastel prints are the perfect table accent for a spring luncheon setting.

Designs | Michele Crawford

Skill Level
Easy

Finished Sizes
Placemat: 12½ x 18½ inches
Table Runner: 10½ x 48½ inches
Napkins: 18 x 18 inches

Materials for Runner & Four Place Settings
44/45-inch-wide fabrics:
- ⅓ yard yellow tone-on-tone print for the placemats and runners
- ¼ yard pink tone-on-tone print for the basket bows
- ¼ yard green tone-on-tone print for the placemats
- ⅓ yard purple tone-on-tone print for the placemats and runner
- ⅓ yard bright pink tone-on-tone print for the placemats and runner
- 2¾ yards multicoloured ribbon plaid for the baskets, backing, runner points and binding
- 1⅛ yards pink floral print for the napkins
- ¾ yard white solid for the basket block backgrounds

1⅔ yards paper-backed fusible web
48 x 60-inch piece cotton batting
Pink and gold rayon embroidery thread
White machine-quilting thread
Temporary spray adhesive

Note: Fabric yardage is based on 40 inches of usable width after preshrinking.

Cutting
Prewash all fabrics and press to remove wrinkles.

From the yellow tone-on-tone print:
- Cut three 2½ x 40-inch strips. From the strips, cut 16 rectangles each 2½ x 4½ inches for the placemats and two strips each 2½ x 10½ inches for the table runner.

From the pink tone-on-tone print:
- Cut one strip 4½ x 27 inches for the basket bows.

From the green tone-on-tone print:
- Cut three strips, each 1½ x 40 inches. From the strips, cut eight strips, each 1½ x 10½ inches for the placemats.

From the purple tone-on-tone print:
- Cut three 2½ x 40-inch strips. From the strips, cut 16 rectangles each 2½ x 4½ inches for the placemats and two strips each 2½ x 10½ inches for the table runner.

From the bright pink:
- Cut three 2½ x 40-inch strips. From the strips, cut 16 rectangles each 2½ x 4½ inches for the placemats and 2 strips each 2½ x 10½ inches for the table runner.

Spring's in the Basket

From the ribbon plaid:
• Cut eight strips each 2½ inches wide for the binding; set aside.

• Cut two 10 x 40-inch strips. From the strips, cut a total of six 10-inch squares for the baskets.

• Cut one strip 10½ inches wide. From the strip, cut two rectangles each 8½ x 10½ inches for the runner points and one 10½ x 12-inch rectangle for the runner backing.

• Cut one 12 x 40-inch strip for the runner backing.

• From the remaining fabric, cut four 13 x 19-inch rectangles for the placemat backings.

Note: If you are using a true plaid or check for the binding, consider cutting bias strips instead for a more noticeable bound edge.

From the pink floral print:
• Cut four 18½-inch squares for the napkins.

From the white solid fabric:
• Cut six 10½-inch squares for the placemats and runner.

From the batting:
• Cut four 13 x 19-inch rectangles for the placemats.

• Cut one 12 x 50-inch strip for the table runner.

From the fusible web:
• Cut six 10-inch squares.

• Cut six 4½-inch squares.

Assembly
Use ¼-inch seam allowances unless otherwise indicated.

For the placemat basket panels, sew a 1½ x 10½-inch green strip to opposite edges of each of four 10½-inch white squares. Press the seams toward the strips.

Referring to Figure 1, arrange the 2½ x 4½-inch purple, yellow and bright pink strips in two rows for each placemat. Sew together and press the seams in one direction. Sew a pieced strip to opposite edges of each basket panel from step 1. Press the seam toward the pieced strips.

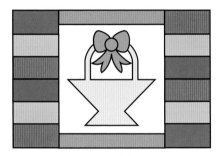

Figure 1
Placemat Layout

For each placemat, apply a light coat of temporary spray adhesive to the wrong side of the 13 x 19-inch ribbon-plaid rectangles and allow to dry. Centre a 13 x 19-inch batting piece on the rectangle and smooth into place. Apply quilt basting spray to the batting and allow to dry. Smooth a pieced placemat in place on top.

With white machine-quilting thread on the machine, stitch in the ditch of the seam around the white square. Machine-stitch ⅛ inch from the raw edges of the placemat. Trim the batting and backing even with the placemat edges.

Trim the two 8½ x 10½-inch rectangles of ribbon plaid as shown in Figure 2.

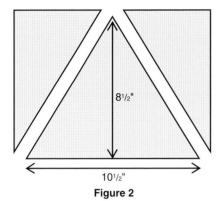

8½"

10½"

Figure 2

Referring to Figure 3, arrange the pieces for the table runner and sew together. Press the seams as directed by the arrows.

For the runner back, sew the 12 x 40-inch and 10½ x 12-inch ribbon plaid rectangles together to make a 12 x 50-inch rectangle for the table runner back. Press.

Layer the runner back, batting and pieced runner using quilting spray adhesive as described for the placemats.

With white machine-quilting thread on the machine, stitch in the ditch around the outer edges of the white squares. Stitch ⅛ inch from the outer edge of the pieced runner and trim the batting and backing even with the runner edges.

Sew the 2½-inch-wide binding strips together using bias seams to make one long strip and press the seams open.

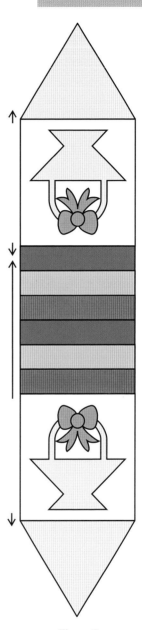

Figure 3
Table Runner Layout

Fold the strip in half lengthwise with wrong sides together and raw edges even and press.

Bind each placemat and the runner, mitring the corners as you go. Press the binding toward the seam allowance, then wrap it over the seam edge to the underside and hand-sew in place, mitring the corners and tacking them in place.

Trace the basket template onto the wrong side of each of the 10-inch squares of fusible web. Following manufacturer's directions, apply the fusible web to the wrong side of each of the six squares of ribbon plaid. Cut out each basket, remove the paper backing and centre each one on a white square on a placemat or the table runner. Fuse in place.

Trace the bow template onto the backing paper of each 4½-inch square of fusible web. Apply the squares to the wrong side of the 4½ x 27-inch strip of pink tone-on-tone. Cut out each bow. Remove the backing paper and position each one on a basket handle (see photo page 43). Fuse in place.

Use gold rayon thread in the needle and yellow all-purpose thread in the bobbin. Adjust the machine for an appliqué stitch and sew around the outer edges of each basket. Change to pink rayon thread in the needle and pink all-purpose thread on the bobbin and stitch around the bows. Stitch around the centre of the bow to make the "knot."

Stipple-quilt the centre strips and the points of the runner. If desired, stipple-quilt in the pieced strips on each placemat.

Make a double narrow hem around the outer edge of each napkin square. ■

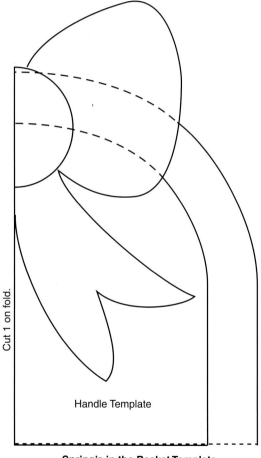

Cut 1 on fold.

Handle Template

Spring's in the Basket Template
Actual Size
Join to basket at dashed line.

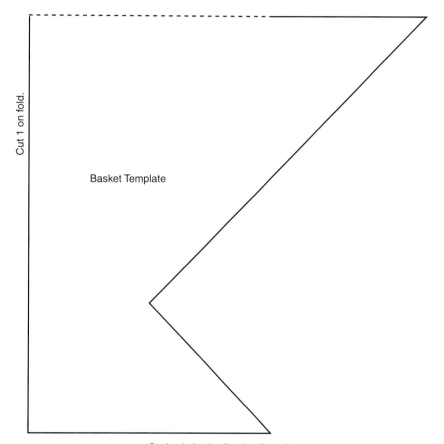

Cut 1 on fold.

Basket Template

Spring's in the Basket Template
Actual Size
Join to handle at dashed line.

VINTAGE CHIC TABLE SET

Soft vintage-inspired fabrics set the mood for this beautiful table setting. Select a large floral print and combine it with a coordinating plaid and stripe.

Designs | Michele Crawford

Skill Level
Easy

Finished Sizes
Table Runner: 12½ x 58 inches
Placemat: 12½ x 18½ inches
Napkin: 18½ x 18½ inches

Materials for Runner & Two Place Settings
44/45-inch-wide fabric:
- 1⅞ yards floral print
- ⅝ yard green mini plaid
- ¼ yard rose ticking stripe

¼ yard of 60-inch-wide natural basket-weave print
½ yard paper-backed fusible web
1¾ yards quilter's fleece
Natural rayon thread
Dark rust and natural machine-quilting thread
3 packages natural wide bias tape
1 package natural woven seam binding
2 green 3-inch long tassels

Placemats

Cutting
From natural basket-weave print:
- Cut two 8½ x 14½-inch rectangles for centres.

From green mini plaid:
- Cut four 2½ x 8½-inch strips and four 2½ x 14½-inch strips for borders.

From rose ticking stripe:
- Cut eight 2½-inch squares for border corners.

From floral print:
- Cut two 12½ x 18½-inch rectangles for backings.

From fleece:
- Cut two 12½ x 18½-inch rectangles.

Assembly
Use ¼ inch seam allowances unless otherwise indicated. Stitch pieces together with right sides together, raw edges even and with matching thread. Press seam allowances open to reduce bulk.

Following Placemat Assembly Diagram (see page 50), stitch a long mini plaid border strip to top and bottom of placemat centre. Press. Stitch a ticking stripe border corner to each end of short mini plaid border strips. Press. Stitch a pieced border strip to each side of placemat centre to complete two 12½ x 18½-inch placemat tops. Press.

Centre fleece on wrong side of floral print rectangle. Centre wrong side of placemat pieced top on fleece.

Vintage Chic Table Set

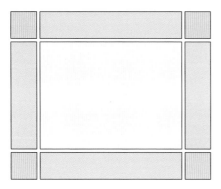

Placemat Assembly Diagram

Pin layers together and hand-baste. Using natural quilting thread, machine quilt in seam around centre rectangle and corner squares. Top-stitch around outside of placemat ⅛ inch from edge.

For binding, stitch wide bias tape around each placemat, mitring corners and overlapping ends.

Turn bias tape to back of each placemat; pin and hand-sew in place.

Appliquéd Design

Cut a ½-inch border around two large floral designs from floral print.

Fuse wrong side of each floral design on paper-backed fusible web. Carefully cut an approximate ⅛-inch border around floral design. Peel off paper back from each floral design, and centre in basket-weave print section of each placemat. This technique is known as *broderie perse*.

Using natural rayon thread in top of sewing machine and matching all-purpose thread in bobbin, machine-appliqué over ⅛-inch seam allowance on each floral design.

Using dark rust machine-quilting thread, machine-stipple in basket-weave print area around each floral design.

Table Runner

Cutting

From natural basket-weave print:
• Cut an 8½ x 24½-inch rectangle for centre.

From green mini plaid:
• Cut two 2½ x 24½-inch strips and two 2½ x 8½-inch strips for borders.

• Cut two 8 x 12½-inch rectangles. Cut rectangles into triangles for runner ends (Figure 1).

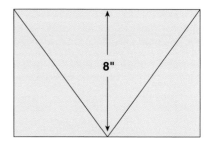

8"

Figure 1

From rose ticking stripe:
• Cut four 2½-inch squares for border corners.

• Cut four 2 x 12½-inch strips for pieced border.

From floral print:
• Cut six 2 x 12½-inch strips.

• Cut one piece 14 x 45 inches and another piece 14 x 15 inches for backing.

Assembly

Use ¼ inch seam allowances unless otherwise indicated. Stitch pieces together with right sides together, raw edges even and with matching thread. Press seam allowances open to reduce bulk.

Table Runner Assembly Diagram

Following Table Runner Assembly Diagram, stitch a long mini plaid border strip to top and bottom of table runner centre. Press. Stitch a ticking strip border corner to each end of short mini plaid border strips. Press. Stitch a pieced strip to each side of table runner centre. Press.

Following Assembly Diagram, alternate stitching three floral print strips with two rose ticking strips to make an 8 x 12½-inch section. Repeat. Press. Stitch a pieced section to each side of bordered table runner centre. Press.

Stitch a mini plaid triangle to each end of pieced section to complete 12½ x 58-inch table runner top.

For table runner backing, stitch 14 x 45-inch piece and 14 x 15-inch piece together to make a long piece. Press seam open.

Centre fleece on wrong side of floral print rectangle. Centre wrong side of table runner top on fleece.

Pin layers together and hand-baste. Using natural machine-quilting thread, machine-quilt in seam around centre rectangle and corner squares. Machine-quilt ⅛ inch from each side of floral print strips in pieced section. Using dark rust machine-quilting thread, machine-stipple

in natural basket-weave rectangle. Topstitch around outside of table runner ⅛ inch in from edge. Trim excess fabric next to table runner top.

For binding, stitch wide bias tape around table runner, mitring corners and overlapping ends. Turn bias tape to back of table runner, pin and hand sew in place.

Sew loop of tassel to wrong side at each end of table runner.

Napkins

Cutting
From floral print:
• Cut two 19-inch squares.

From woven seam binding:
• Cut two 18-inch lengths.

Assembly
Press raw edge of each square under ¼ inch. Turn pressed edge under ¼ inch and topstitch with natural thread.

Tie a length of seam binding in a bow around each napkin. ■

COUNTRY KITCHEN SET

Brighten your breakfast table with this vintage runner-and-hot-pad set stitched in country colours.

Designs | Cheryl Fall

Skill Level
Beginner

Finished Sizes
Runner: 15⅛ x 26½ inches
Hot Pad: 8½ x 8½ inches

Materials
44/45-inch-wide cotton fabrics:
> ¼ yard each blue gingham, red gingham, green print and white-on-white print
> ⅓ yard of multicoloured print for centre areas
> ⅓ yard of blue print for border
> ½ yard of coordinating solid blue for backing

½ yard low-loft cotton batting
Paper-backed fusible web
2 yellow buttons
¾-inch plastic ring
Red and mint green rayon thread
Clear monofilament thread
Red baby rickrack
Red extra-wide double-fold bias tape

Cutting
From multicoloured print:
• Cut one piece 11½ x 18½ inches for runner centre.

• Cut one piece 4½ x 4½ inches for hot pad centre.

From blue gingham:
• Cut 22 pieces each 1½ x 1½ inches.

From white-on-white print:
• Cut 22 pieces each 1½ x 1½ inches.

From blue print:
• Cut two pieces each 2½ x 18½ inches and two pieces each 2½ x 15½ inches for runner borders.

• Cut two pieces each 2½ x 8½ inches and two pieces each 2½ x 4½ inches for hot pad borders.

From solid blue:
• Cut one piece 16 x 27 inches for runner backing.

• Cut one piece 9 x 9 inches for hot pad backing.

Country Kitchen Set

Appliqués

Fuse web to wrong side of green print fabric and red gingham fabric. Using templates on page 55, trace three right-facing leaves and two left-facing leaves on paper side of green print. Trace two flowers on paper side of red gingham. Cut out leaves and flowers.

Table Runner Assembly

Use ¼-inch seam allowances and stitch pieces right sides together unless otherwise indicated.

Use all-purpose thread for construction unless otherwise stated.

Stitch blue gingham and white-on-white 1½-inch squares together to make two checkerboard strips.

Stitch one checkered strip to each short end of runner centre piece. Stitch long blue print border pieces to long edges of runner centre. Stitch short blue print border pieces to ends of runner centre (Figure 1).

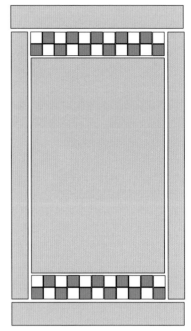

Figure 1

Arrange and fuse flowers and leaves on runner centre and hot pad centre as shown in photo (see page 53) or as desired. Using rayon thread, satin-stitch around edges of each appliqué.

Layer runner top with batting and backing fabric. Pin or baste layers together. Using monofilament thread, quilt along all seam lines. Quilt ¼ inch from seam lines inside borders. Quilt parallel lines across runner centre, spacing stitching lines 1 inch apart.

Stitch ⅛ inch from raw edges on runner. Trim away excess batting and backing fabric. Bind outer edge of runner with bias tape using monofilament thread.

Using a narrow zigzag setting, stitch rickrack along border seam lines and checkered strips seam lines.

Hand-stitch a button to centre of each flower.

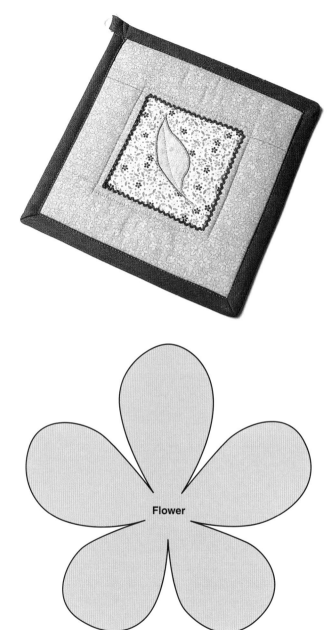

Hot Pad Assembly

Stitch short hot pad border pieces to opposite edges of hot pad centre. Stitch long hot pad border pieces to remaining sides of hot pad centre and short border pieces.

Using hot pad pieces, assemble top in same manner as runner top. Layer top, backing and fleece, and baste edges together.

Appliqué leaf at centre of hot pad top in same manner as leaves on runner.

Using a narrow zigzag setting, stitch rickrack along seam lines of centre. Stitch ⅛ inch from raw edges on runner. Trim away excess batting and backing fabric.

Bind outer edge of hot pad with bias tape, leaving a 2-inch tail at the top corner. Place plastic ring on tail, fold the tail to the back of the corner to make a hanging loop and tack in place by hand or machine. ■

Flower

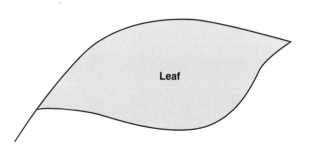

Leaf

CHEERY YO-YOS TABLE SET

You will set the table for a delightful tea party for two with this charming project.

Designs | Chris Malone

Skill Level
Easy

Finished Sizes
Tea Cozy: 11 x 13 inches
Placemat: 12½ x 16½ inches
Napkin: 15 x 15 inches
Napkin Ring: 2¼ x 4¾ inches

Materials for Tea Cozy & Two Place Settings
44/45-inch-wide cotton fabrics:
  1 yard light green floral print
  ½ yard coordinating dark green floral print
  ⅝ yard coordinating dark rose print
  ¼ yard coordinating medium rose print
  ¼ yard coordinating medium green print
Assorted scraps of coordinating blues, golds and
  light rose prints
12 x 30-inch rectangle low-loft batting
14 x 40-inch rectangle high-loft batting
1 yard ivory piping
1 yard ivory single-fold bias tape
4 (⅞-inch) ivory buttons
8 (⅝-inch) ivory buttons
11 inches ¾-inch-wide elastic
Ecru hand-quilting thread (optional)
Dark green embroidery floss
Embroidery needle

Air-soluble marking pen
Permanent fabric glue
Zipper foot

Tea Cozy

Cutting
From light green floral print:
• Cut one 11½ x 14-inch rectangle for the tea cozy front. Fold in half so it measures 7 x 11½ inches. Round the corners opposite the fold (Figure 1). *Note: A dinner plate is a good guide for this cut.* Using the cozy front as a pattern, cut two more cozy shapes from light green floral print for the lining, one from dark green floral print for the cozy back and two from low-loft batting.

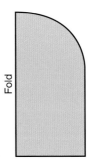

Fig. 1
Round one corner of cozy
as shown.

Cheery Yo-Yos Table Set

From assorted print scraps:
• Cut two 4½-inch-diameter circles, five 4-inch circles and three 3-inch circles for the yo-yo flowers.

From medium green print:
• Cut four 4-inch squares, three 3½-inch squares and four 3-inch squares for the leaves.

Assembly
Use ¼-inch seam allowances unless otherwise indicated.

Referring to the photo (see page 57), use the air-soluble marking pen to draw freehand lines for vines on the right side of the cozy front. Embroider along the lines with stem stitches, using an embroidery needle and three strands of dark green embroidery floss.

Place one cozy lining wrong side up with the batting on top. Smooth the cozy front in place with the right side up. Mark a 2-inch diagonal grid for quilting on the cozy front. Pin and baste the layers together. Prepare the cozy back in the same manner.

Quilt on the marked lines by hand or machine.

With raw edges even, pin piping to the curved edge of the cozy front. Attach the zipper foot and machine-baste close to the piping cord.

Pin the cozy front and back together with right sides facing and raw edges even. Stitching from the wrong side of the cozy front so you can see the basting, stitch the layers together, positioning the stitches just inside the machine basting. Zigzag- or serge-finish the seam edges together. Turn right side out.

Unfold the bias tape and turn under the short end. Beginning in the centre of the back raw edge of the cozy, pin the bias tape to the lower edge of the cozy. Overlap the end when you reach it and trim the excess. Stitch in the fold line. Wrap the bias tape over the raw edge to the inside of the cozy and slipstitch in place.

To make a yo-yo flower, finger-press a ⅛-inch hem around the outer edge of a fabric circle and hand-baste in place. To gather the circle into a flower, draw up the stitches and arrange with the hole in the flower centre (Figure 2). Take several stitches to secure. Make 10 yo-yo flowers.

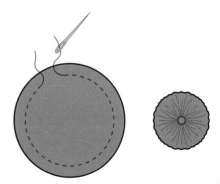

Fig. 2
Make flowers as shown.

To make a leaf, fold a fabric square in half, wrong sides together. Fold the corners down to meet in the centre with all raw edges even to form a triangle (Figure 3). Hand-baste through all layers ⅛ inch from the raw edges. Draw up the thread to gather into a leaf shape. Make 11 leaves.

Fig. 3
Make leaves as shown.

Arrange the flowers along the vines on the tea cozy front and pin in place. Sew yo-yos in place with a button in the centre of each one. Use two large buttons for the two largest flowers and small buttons for the remaining flowers.

Arrange leaves around flowers as desired with the raw edges under the flower edges. Glue leaves in place under the flowers.

Placemats

Cutting
From dark green floral print:
• Cut two 8 x 12-inch rectangles for the centre-front panels.

• Cut two 13 x 17-inch rectangles for the backing.

From medium rose print:
• Cut two 3 x 8-inch strips and two 3 x 17-inch strips for the borders.

From high-loft batting:
• Cut two 13 x 17-inch rectangles.

Assembly
Sew short border strips to opposite sides of each centre panel. Press the seams toward the borders. Add the long border strips to the centre panel and press the seams toward the borders.

Arrange a batting rectangle on the work surface with the backing on top, right side up. Place the placemat front facedown on the backing with raw edges even. Pin. Stitch ¼ inch from the raw edges, leaving a 6-inch opening at one edge. Trim the batting close to the stitching and clip the corners. Turn right side out through the opening and press, turning in the opening edges. Slipstitch the opening closed.

Hand- or machine-quilt by stitching in the ditch of the border seamlines.

Napkins

Cutting
From light green floral print:
• Cut two 15-inch squares.

From dark rose print:
• Cut two 18½-inch squares.

Assembly
Turn under and press ½ inch around each 18½-inch square. Place the squares facedown on the work surface and centre a green floral square on top of each one with right side up. Pin in place.

Turn the napkin square over the green floral square with the folds along the raw edges. Make diagonal folds in the napkin fabric to mitre the corners (Figure 4). Trim excess fabric inside the mitre to eliminate bulk. Slipstitch the mitred fold to the napkin at each corner. Machine-stitch close to the inner folded edge of the napkin.

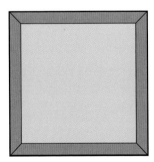

Fig. 4
Mitre placemat corners as shown.

Napkin Rings

Cutting
From medium green print:
• Cut two 2¼ x 9½-inch strips.

Assembly
Fold each strip in half lengthwise with right sides together and stitch ¼ inch from the long edges. Press the seams open and turn tubes right side out. Centre the seams on the back of the tubes and press.

Insert a 5½-inch-long piece of elastic into each tube, gathering the tube on the elastic so the ends are even with the tube raw edges. Pin. Fold the tube in half with the seamed side inside and stitch the short ends together. Press the seam open.

Make two large yo-yo flowers and four large leaves as instructed for the Tea Cozy.

For each napkin ring, sew a ⅞-inch ivory button to the centre of a flower and then to the elasticized band, covering the seam. Apply glue to the gathered end of each leaf and tuck under a flower on each side with the leaves parallel to the elastic band (see photo). ■

SCALLOPED TABLE TOPPER

This tablecloth is the perfect fit for your favourite round table. Choose coordinating fabrics for a custom tailored look.

Designs | Ann Brown

Skill Level
Intermediate

Finished Size
Photographed model fits a 42-inch round table with a 5-inch drop border. To make a different-size table topper, follow the measuring and pattern information in the instructions and adjust the fabric amounts accordingly.

Materials
58/60-inch-wide decorator fabrics:
- 1¼ yards of solid woven pattern for tabletop
- 1¼ yards of muslin or solid broadcloth for lining
- 1½ yards of toile or desired print for scallop drop border
- 1 yard of stripe or print to coordinate with toile for piping

7 yards 4mm cord for piping
Unprinted newspaper, pattern-tracing fabric or any other large tracing material
Water-soluble fabric marking pen
Piping foot or zipper foot

Cutting
For tabletop and lining pattern, lay paper or pattern fabric on tabletop and draw a line along edge of the table. Add ½-inch seam allowance around first line and cut out circle.

From solid woven pattern:
- Using tabletop pattern, cut one circle.

From muslin:
- Using tabletop pattern, cut one circle.

From toile:
- Cut six 6-inch-wide strips from selvage to selvage. For larger table, cut enough additional strips to get length needed for scalloped border strips.

From coordinating stripe or print:
- Cut into 1½-inch-wide bias strips for piping.

Assembly
Use ½-inch for seam allowances and stitch pieces right sides together unless otherwise indicated.

Stitch bias strips end-to-end, forming one long strip. Fold bias strip around cord and using piping foot or zipper foot, stitch close to cord.

For each border strip, stitch three toile fabric strips end-to-end, forming two long strips. Press seams open. Trim each long strip using border strip measurement.

Enlarge scallop pattern (see page 62) 200 per cent. Allowing ½ inch at each end for seam allowance (Figure 1), trace scallop pattern along bottom edge on wrong side of one border strip, adjusting width of scallops to fit as needed. *Note: Depending on the circumference of your table, a few of the scallops may need to be slightly wider or narrower so it will have a continuous flow from the last scallop to the first scallop on the edge.*

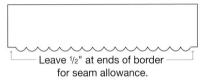

Leave ½" at ends of border
for seam allowance.

Figure 1

Pin the two border strips right sides together and cut both layers along the marked line at the same time so the scalloped edges will match when they are stitched together. Make a dot with a water-soluble pen at the quarter marks on the strips to help match them properly.

On one of the border strips, matching raw edges, baste piping to scalloped edge, clipping the seam allowance on the cord every ½ inch or as needed to form smooth curves.

Stitch curved bottom edges of border strips together. Trim and clip seam allowance. Turn right side out and press. Refold partially assembled border strips right sides together and stitch short ends of strips together, forming a ring. Press seam open. Turn right side out.

Stitch tabletop piece to scallop border, making certain to catch only one raw edge. Stitch tabletop lining to remaining raw edge of scallop border underside, leaving a 12-inch opening for turning. Trim seam to ¼ inch. Turn right side out and hand-stitch opening closed. ■

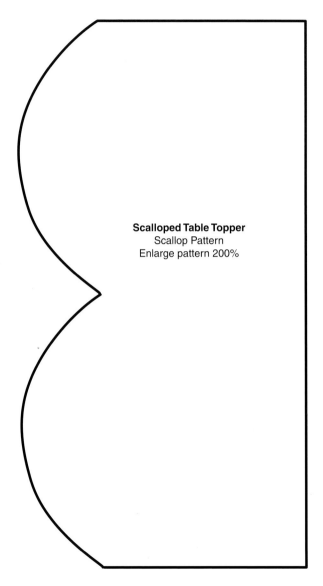

Scalloped Table Topper
Scallop Pattern
Enlarge pattern 200%

Scalloped Table Topper

Spring in Provence Table Toppings

Add a bit of French flair to your springtime table settings. Small figurative prints and coordinating border stripes in sun-drenched colours add up to a warm ambience.

Designs | Carol Zentgraf

Skill Level
Easy

Finished Sizes
Tablecloth: 61 x 61 inches
Napkin: 20 x 20 inches
Napkin Ring: 1½ x 7 inches

Materials for Runner, Two Napkins & Napkin Rings
60/63-inch-wide cotton fabric*:
   2 yards 6 French Provençal stripe
   ⅔ yard French Provençal coordinating print
3 x 7-inch strip heavyweight fusible interfacing
   for each napkin ring
¾-inch decorative button for each napkin ring
Narrow strips of fusible web (optional)
*For narrower fabrics and larger tables, you will need two lengths of fabric to piece into a square of the desired size before hemming.

Cutting
From French Provençal stripe:
• Cut a square panel, as large as possible, with cut edges perpendicular to the lines of the printed stripe.

• For each napkin ring, cut a 3½ x 7½-inch strip, centring printed stripe.

From French Provençal coordinating print:
• For each napkin, cut a 22 x 22-inch square.

Assembly
Referring to Mitring Double-Turned Corners on page 70, hem each edge of the tablecloth square with a ½-inch-wide double hem. Stitch each hem in place ⅜ inch from pressed edge. Repeat with napkin squares.

Centre a strip of interfacing on the wrong side of each napkin-ring strip and fuse in place following manufacturer's directions. Fold the strip in half lengthwise with right sides together and stitch ¼ inch from long raw edges, leaving a 2-inch-long opening in the centre of the seam. Press the seam to one side.

Centre seam line in fabric tube and stitch ¼ inch from each short edge (Figure 1). Turn right side out through opening and press. Slipstitch opening closed, or tuck a narrow strip of fusible web between the opening layers and fuse opening closed.

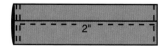

Figure 1

Spring in Provence Table Toppings

To finish each napkin ring, make a buttonhole 1 inch from one end. Sew a button in place ½ inch from opposite end. Fold napkins as desired and button the rings around them. ■

Mitring Double-Turned Corners

For projects, such as napkins, where both sides will be visible, mitring the turned corner provides a neat finished look.

To mitre each corner for a ½-inch-wide finished doubled hem, make a mark 2 inches from each side of the corner. Use a straightedge to draw a line connecting the marks to create a 45-degree triangle at each corner. Draw lines ½ inch from the raw edge at each set of adjacent corners to mark the first fold line (Figure 2).

Make a fold at each corner with the ends of the lines matching. Beginning at the fold, stitch on the line, ending the stitching precisely at the marked fold line (½ inch from the raw edge). Trim the corner ¼ inch from the stitching as shown in Figure 3.

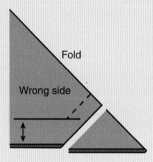

Figure 3

Turn right side out and press, turning the raw edge under ½ inch (Figure 4). Topstitch the hem in place ⅜ inch from the outer edges. ■

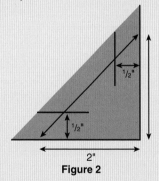

Figure 2

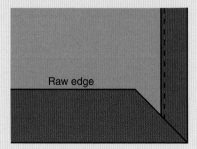

Figure 4

SUMMER GARDEN

*Complementary colours blue and yellow
make a perfect summer runner.*

Design | Toby Lischko

Skill Level
Beginner

Finished Size
54 x 27 inches

Materials
44/45-inch-wide fabric:
    ⅜ yard yellow floral
    ¾ yard yellow print
    1 yard blue print
    1⅜ yards blue floral
Backing 56 x 29 inches
Batting 56 x 29 inches
Quilting thread

Cutting
From yellow floral:
• Cut one 9½-inch strip the width of the fabric; subcut strip into four 9½-inch A squares.

From yellow print:
• Cut three 5-inch strips the width of the fabric; subcut strips into (20) 5-inch D squares. Mark a diagonal line from corner to corner on the wrong side of each square.

• Cut two 5⅜ x 5⅜-inch (F) squares. Cut each square in half on one diagonal to make four (F) triangles.

From blue print:
• Cut two 5-inch strips the width of the fabric; subcut strips into (16) 5-inch B squares. Draw a diagonal line from corner to corner on the wrong side of each square.

• Cut two 9½-inch strips the width of the fabric; subcut strips into (10) 5-inch C pieces.

From blue floral:
• Cut two 5 x 45½-inch (H) strips along the length of the fabric.

• Cut two 5 x 18½-inch (G) strips along the length of the fabric.

• Cut four 5⅜ x 5⅜-inch (E) squares. Cut each square in half on one diagonal to make eight (E) triangles.

Unit Assembly
Referring to Figure 1, stitch B along the marked line to opposite corners of A; trim seams to ¼ inch and press B to the right side. Repeat on the remaining corners of A to complete an A-B unit. Repeat to make four A-B units.

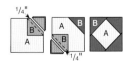

Figure 1

Referring to Figure 2, stitch D to one end of C; trim seam to ¼ inch and press D to the right side. Repeat on the opposite end of C to complete a C-D unit. Repeat to make 10 C-D units.

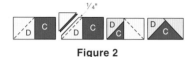

Figure 2

Sew E to F along the diagonal; press seam toward E. Repeat to make four E-F units.

Runner Assembly

Join four A-B units with two C-D units to make the centre row as shown in Figure 3; press seams in one direction.

Figure 3

Join four C-D units with two E-F units to make the top row as shown in Figure 4; press seams in the opposite direction from the centre row. Repeat to make the bottom row.

Figure 4

Join the rows to complete the pieced centre; press seams toward the centre row.

Sew H strips to opposite long sides of the pieced centre; press seams toward H strips.

Sew E to each end of each G strip; press seams toward E. Repeat to make two E-G strips.

Sew the E-G strips to each short end of the pieced centre referring to the Placement Diagram for positioning; press seams toward the E-G strips to complete the runner top.

Lay the batting on a flat surface; place the backing right side up on the batting. Place the pieced top right sides together with the layered batting and backing; smooth and pin to hold.

Sew all around the outside edges, leaving a 6-inch opening on one side. Trim backing even with top and batting close to stitching.

Turn right side out through the opening; press opening seams under ¼ inch; hand-stitch opening closed.

Quilt as desired by hand or machine to finish. ■

Summer Garden
Placement Diagram
54" x 27"

Summer Garden

ENGLISH COTTAGE KITCHEN

English cottage gardens provided the inspiration for this lovely floral table setting. Stitch the entire set for a beautiful layered look or select just one or two pieces to spruce up your table.

Designs | Michele Crawford

Skill Level
Beginner

Finished Sizes
Tablecloth: 58 inches in diameter
Square Table Topper: 36 x 36 inches
Round Topper: 18½ inches in diameter
Napkin: 20 x 20 inches
Chair Cover: custom fit

Materials for Table Accessories & Two Chair Covers
Purchased home decor pattern that includes
   chair back cover
42-inch-wide fabric:
     1¼ yards large floral print
     1 yard coordinating floral print
     3⅓ yards checkerboard print
     1⅔ yards dots print
½ yard paper-backed fusible web
1 yard fleece
Rayon thread
1 package natural covered piping
1 yard ¼-inch off-white twisted cord

Cutting
From large floral print:
• Cut one 37 x 37-inch square for square table topper.

• Cut seven flower motifs from fabric print for appliqués.

From coordinating floral print:
Note: Adjust purchased pattern piece to fit chair, allowing for a ¼-inch seam allowance.

• Cut four chair cover pieces for fronts and backs.

From checkerboard print:
• Cut one piece 42 x 60 inches and one piece 18 x 60 inches for tablecloth.

• Cut two 18½-inch-diameter circles for round topper.

• Cut three 2¼ x 60-inch strips for napkin binding.

• Cut four 2¼ x 60-inch strips for chair-cover binding.

From dots print:
• Cut one 10½ x 10½-inch square for round topper.

• Cut two 1½-inch-wide bias strips the width of the fabric for round topper binding.

English Cottage Kitchen

- Cut two 20 x 20-inch squares for napkins.

- Cut four 3½ x 55-inch strips for chair cover ties.

From fleece:
- Cut one 18½-inch diametre circle for round topper.

- Use adjusted pattern to cut two chair cover pieces.

From paper–backed fusible web:
- Cut one 10-inch-diametre circle for round topper.

From twisted cord:
- Cut two 18-inch lengths.

Assembly
Unless otherwise indicated, use ¼ inch seam allowances, and stitch pieces with matching thread, right sides together and raw edges even.

Tablecloth
Stitch the two checkerboard rectangles together to make a 60-inch square. Press seam open. Measure and cut square into a 60-inch-diameter circle. Press raw edge under ¼ inch. Turn pressed edge under ¼ inch and topstitch.

Square Table Topper
Press raw edge of large floral print square under ¼ inch. Turn pressed edge under ¼ inch and topstitch.

Round Topper
Apply 10-inch fusible-web circle to wrong side of 10½ x 10½-inch dots print square. Cut around the circle. Peel off paper backing, and then centre and fuse circle to one checkerboard circle for topper front.

Apply fusible web to wrong sides of five flower motifs for appliqué. Cut around each motif and peel off paper back. Centre one motif in dots circle, and other four motifs evenly spaced around dots circle, overlapping the checkerboard circle. Fuse in place.

Place second checkerboard circle right side down, fleece circle on top and wrong side of topper front over fleece. Pin layers together. With rayon thread in top of sewing machine and matching all-purpose thread in bobbin, use a machine satin stitch to appliqué each motif and the raw edge of dots circle between the motifs.

With all-purpose thread, machine stipple in the dots circle between the motifs and in checkerboard circle. Topstitch around checkerboard circle ⅛ inch from edge.

Stitch ends of dots bias binding strips together to make one long strip. Press long edge under ¼ inch. Stitch binding strip around checkerboard circle overlapping ends. Turn binding to back of circle and hand-stitch in place.

Napkins

Stitch checkerboard binding strips together to make one long strip. Press seams open. With wrong sides together, fold strip in half lengthwise. Stitch binding strip around each napkin square, mitring corners and overlapping the ends. Turn binding to back of square and hand-stitch in place.

Apply fusible web to backs of two flower motif for appliqué. Cut around motif. Centre each motif 1½ inches from one corner of napkin. Fuse in place. Machine-appliqué motifs as done for round table topper. Knot each end of 18-inch length of twisted cord. Tie each cord in a bow around napkin.

Chair Covers

Fold each 3½ x 55-inch dots-print strip for ties in half lengthwise, right sides together. Sew along one long edge of each piece. Turn right side out and press.

Fold one end of each strip into a triangle, and stitch open edges together; turn to conceal seam allowance. Make a small pleat in opposite end of each tie; baste in place.

On right side of each of two chair cover pieces, use a zipper foot to stitch piping around curved edge. (These will be the chair cover fronts. Remaining chair cover pieces will be the backs.) With raw edges even, baste pleated end of each tie to right side of front piece ½ inch from bottom edge.

Place one chair cover front right side down. Place a fleece chair cover piece on top, and the wrong side of a chair cover back on top. Pin layers together. Repeat with the remaining chair cover front and back pieces to make a second unit. Using zipper foot, stitch around curved edge of each unit close to piping. Clip seam allowance. Turn right side out.

Stitch two checkerboard chair cover binding strips together to make one long strip. Press seam open. Fold strip in half lengthwise with wrong sides together and press. Sew strip around bottom open edge of chair cover overlapping ends. Turn strip to inside of chair cover and hand-stitch in place. Repeat for second chair cover. ■

MOSAIC PLACEMATS

Broken china dishes provided the inspiration for these placemats. Duplicate the look of tile and grout lines with cut-fabric pieces in your decor colours, accented by a cream background.

Design | Ann Brown

Skill Level
Beginner

Finished Size
13½ x 19 inches

Materials
½ yard 58-inch-wide off-white medium-weight duck cloth
½ yard print decorator fabric for bias binding
Variety of coordinating print scraps
1 yard paper-backed fusible web
½ yard fusible fleece
Off-white sewing thread
No. 18 machine needle
Sewing machine with zigzag feature

Cutting
From cotton duck fabric:
• Cut two ovals each 13½ x 19 inches.

From fusible fleece:
• Cut one oval 13½ x 19 inches.

From decorator fabric:
• Cut bias strips 1½ inches wide. Stitch strips end to end, forming one long strip to fit around edge of oval. Press strip in half lengthwise.

Assembly
Fuse fleece to wrong side of one oval of fabric for placemat back.

For placemat top, fuse fusible webbing to wrong side of fabric scraps and remove paper backing. Cut an irregular shape from one fabric scrap and place at centre of second fabric oval on right side. Continue to cut and place irregular shapes around oval, leaving a space between fabric shapes from ½ inch to ¾ inch. Fuse shapes in place.

Set machine for a zigzag with a narrow stitch length and width. Stitch around outer edge of placemat top and around edge of each fabric shape.

With wrong sides together, pin and baste placemat top and back together.

Set machine for straight stitch. Using a ¼-inch seam allowance, stitch bias strip to top. Fold bias to back, turning raw edge under ⅜ inch. Pin in place. Stitch in the ditch from the top, catching the folded edge of the bias strip on the back side. ∎

Mosaic Placemats

SUMMER BRIGHT TABLECLOTH

Cover your picnic table with this bright idea for a tablecloth. Store picnic necessities in the pockets, and keep the cloth from blowing away with a weighted tassel at each corner.

Design | Lynn Weglarz

Skill Level
Beginner

Finished Size
52½ x 93 inches

Materials
54-inch-wide woven fabric:
    3 yards bright print for tablecloth and binding
    ⅜ yard coordinating solid for pockets
1-inch bias tape maker
Optional: ½-inch paper-backed fusible tape
For tassels:
    4 (1-inch) buttons
    assorted yarns to match fabric
    4 (¾-ounce) fishing weights
    3½ x 2½-inch lightweight cardboard

Cutting
From bright print for tablecloth:
• Cut one 54 x 95-inch piece.

• Cut 2-inch strips on the bias the width of the fabric to make 105-inch length when joined.

From coordinating solid for pockets:
• Cut two 6-inch strips the width of the fabric.

Assembly
Use ¼-inch seam allowances unless otherwise indicated.

Sew together bias strips (Figure 1). Trim and press seams. Pull strip through bias tape maker (Figure 2), pressing with iron as you pull it through, to make 105 inches of bias tape. Favor-press tape to make one side a bit wider than the other (Figure 3).

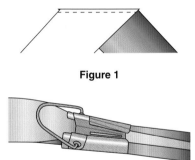

Figure 1

Figure 2

Figure 3

With wider side of bias tape on the wrong side, sew bias tape to one long edge of each 6-inch-wide strip of solid fabric for pocket.

Summer Bright Tablecloth

Place each pocket on one end of tablecloth with wrong side of pocket against right side of tablecloth and raw edges even. Pin and baste.

Stitch a ½-inch double hem in raw edges. Option: Fuse paper-backed fusible tape on wrong side of tablecloth along all edges. Peel paper from short sides. Cut out corner fabric (Figure 4), and then fuse edge to tape. Repeat for remaining edges. Turn under fused edge and topstitch in place.

Figure 4

Referring to stitching diagram, stitch to create pockets (Figure 5).

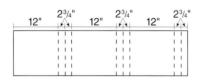

Figure 5

Weighted Tassels

Make one tassel for each corner of the tablecloth.

Thread a 9-inch strand of yarn through one of the fishing weights (Figure 6). Set aside.

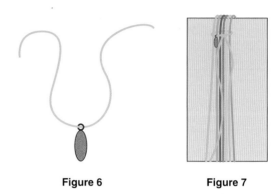

Figure 6   **Figure 7**

Wrap remaining yarn around cardboard about five times, or until cardboard has the desired coverage, beginning and ending with yarn ends at bottom of cardboard.

Slip end of weighted yarn strand under yarn on cardboard and tie off at the top (Figure 7). Tie ends of weighted yarn to form a top loop for attaching to tablecloth. Trim close to knot.

Cut loops at bottom of cardboard. Tie another length of yarn around tassel to create the head of the tassel. *Note: The top of the fishing weight should be in this head.* Trim ends of tassel as desired.

Sew a button to each corner of the tablecloth. Attach tassels by slipping loops over buttons. ∎

CARIBBEAN BREEZE

Sail away to summer relaxation with this quilted table topper and matching tea set. Invite friends and family to enjoy an afternoon outdoor tea party.

Designs | Carolyn Vagts

Skill Level
Beginner

Quilted Table Topper

Finished Size
25 x 25 inches

Materials
44/45-inch-wide lightweight woven fabric:
- 2 yards lime print for centre, backing, borders and binding
- ⅛ yard blue print for corners
- ⅛ yard each 8 different fabrics in teals, blues, greens and yellows for border stripes
- 30 x 30-inch piece batting

Cutting
From lime print:
- Cut one 16½ x 16½-inch square for centre.

- Cut one 30 x 30-inch square for backing.

- Cut four 2-inch strips the width of the fabric. Subcut into two 22½-inch-long strips for short borders and two 26-inch-long strips for long borders.

- Cut three 2½-inch strips the width of the fabric for binding.

From blue print:
- Cut four 3½ x 3½-inch squares for corners.

From each of the eight fabrics for border stripes:
- Cut two 1½-inch strips the width of the fabric. Separate into two groups with one strip of each colour in each group.

Assembly
Use ¼-inch-wide seam allowances unless otherwise indicated.

Using scant ¼-inch-wide seam allowances, sew groups of eight fabric strips together to make two 8½-inch-wide stripe units (Figure 1). *Note: Set one stripe unit aside for use in other projects.*

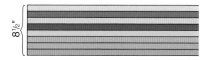

Figure 1

Subcut one unit into eight 3½ x 8½-inch units (Figure 2).

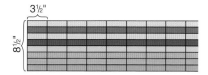

Figure 2

Sew subcut units together in pairs to make four 3½ x 16½-inch units (Figure 3).

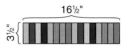

Figure 3

Sew one 3½ x 16½-inch unit to each of two opposite sides of lime centre square. Sew a blue 3½-inch corner square to each end of each remaining 16½-inch unit; sew to remaining sides of lime centre square (Figure 4) to make a 22½ x 22½-inch centre square.

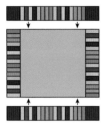 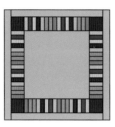

Figure 4   **Figure 5**

Sew lime short border strips to top and bottom of the centre square. Sew lime long border strips to the sides of the centre square (Figure 5).

Sandwich batting between backing and pieced top; quilt as desired. Trim batting and backing even with quilt top edges. Bind edges using the 2½-inch-wide strips.

Tea Cozy

Finished Size
Approximately 11½ x 10 inches

Materials
44/45-inch-wide lightweight woven fabric:
⅓ yard lime print
⅓ yard coordinating print for lining
Reserved stripe unit from Quilted Table Topper
Scraps yellow fabric for appliqués
⅓ yard batting or equivalent
Buttons:
1 yellow 1¼-inch
2 blue ⅞-inch
2 green ⅝-inch
1 yellow ⅝-inch
1 green ⅜-inch
Paper-backed fusible web

Cutting
From lime print:
Note: Cozy template is on page 85. Flower appliqué templates are on page 86.

• Cut four cozy pieces.

From coordinated print for lining:
• Cut four cozy pieces.

From batting:
• Cut four cozy pieces.

From reserved stripe unit:
• Cut four 8½ x 2½-inch stripe units.

From scraps yellow fabric for appliqués:
• Apply fusible web to fabric. Use appliqué templates to cut one each large, medium and small flower appliqué.

Caribbean Breeze

Assembly

Use ¼-inch seam allowances unless otherwise indicated.

Fuse flower appliqués onto two lime print cozy pieces (Figure 6).

Figure 6   **Figure 7**

Pin batting cozy pieces to wrong sides of lime print cozy pieces. Stitch around all sides using a scant ¼-inch seam allowance (Figure 7).

Topstitch around edges of flower appliqués. Quilt each cozy piece as desired.

Sew two cozy pieces with flowers right sides together on one curved edge. Repeat with two remaining cozy pieces. Sew both cozy units together in one long, curved seam (Figure 8).

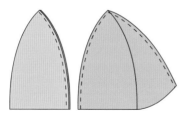

Figure 8

Layer ⅝-inch green buttons on ⅞-inch blue buttons and the ⅜-inch green button on the ⅝-inch yellow button;

sew to centres of flowers. Sew 1¼-inch yellow button to top of cozy. Sew lining cozy pieces together in same manner as for lime print pieces.

With wrong sides together, insert cozy lining into cozy, matching seams. Pin in place. Sew together around bottom raw edge using a scant ¼-inch seam allowance.

Sew the four 8½ x 2½-inch stripe units together to make one long 2½-inch-wide strip (Figure 9). Use strip to bind raw edge of cozy.

Figure 9

Napkins

Finished Size
14 x 14 inches

Materials
44/45-inch-wide lightweight woven fabric:
    1¼ yards lime print
Scraps yellow fabric for appliqués
Paper-backed fusible web
4 blue ½-inch buttons

Cutting
Note: Flower appliqué templates are on page 86.

From lime print:
• Cut eight 14½ x 14½-inch squares for napkins.

From scraps yellow fabric for appliqués:
• Apply fusible web to fabric. Cut four large flower appliqués.

Assembly

Use ¼-inch-wide seam allowances.

Referring to photo (see page 81) for placement, fuse one large flower appliqué in the corner of each of four 14½-inch napkin squares. Straight-stitch around edges of flowers. Sew a button in the centre of each flower.

With right sides together, sew one appliquéd square to one plain square, leaving a 2-inch opening on one side for turning.

Turn right side out and press. Slipstitch opening closed and topstitch a ⅛-inch seam around edges (Figure 10).

Figure 10

Scented Hot Pad

Finished Size

7 x 7 inches

Materials

44/45-inch-wide lightweight woven fabric:
    ½ yard lime print
Reserved stripe unit from Quilted Table Topper
2 (10-inch) squares batting
Scent pellets or rice

Cutting

From lime print:

• Cut one 10-inch square for back.

• Cut a 2-inch strip the width of the fabric. Subcut into two 4½-inch-long strips for short borders and two 7½-inch-long strips for long borders.

• Cut two 2½-inch strips the width of the fabric for binding.

• Cut two 5½ x 5½-inch squares for scent-pellet bag.

From reserved stripe unit:

• Cut one 4½ x 4½-inch square on the diagonal (Figure 11).

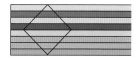

Figure 11

Assembly

Use ¼-inch seam allowances.

Sew short borders to top and bottom edges of the diagonal square unit; sew long borders to remaining edges (Figure 12).

Figure 12

Filled

Figure 13

With right sides together, sew 5½-inch squares together, leaving a 2-inch opening on one side for filling. Fill with scent pellets or rice and stitch closed (Figure 13).

Layer hot pad as follows with raw edges even: 10-inch lime back (right side down), one piece batting, filled bag (centred), second piece batting, pieced top. Pin layers together and stitch in the ditch around the border. Trim to a 9½-inch square.

Bind raw edges with 2½-inch-wide strips, mitring corners.

Coasters

Finished Size
5 x 5 inches

Materials
44/45-inch-wide lightweight woven fabric:
⅝ yard blue print
Reserved stripe unit from Quilted Table Topper
4 (6 x 6-inch) squares batting

Cutting
From blue print:
• Cut three 1¼-inch strips the width of the fabric. Subcut strips into eight 3½-inch lengths for short borders and eight 5-inch lengths for long borders.

• Cut four 6 x 6-inch squares for backs.

• Cut four 2½-inch strips the width of the fabric for binding.

From reserved stripe unit:
• Cut four 3½ x 3½-inch squares on the diagonal (Figure 14).

Figure 14

Assembly
Sew short border pieces to top and bottom of each 3½-inch diagonal strip unit. Sew long border strips to sides of each unit (Figure 15).

Figure 15

Layer batting squares between pieced tops and back pieces. Pin layers together and stitch in the ditch around border seam to quilt. Trim to 5 x 5 inches.

Bind edges using 2½-inch strips.

Tea Bag Holder

Finished Size
3¼ x 3¼ inches

Materials
44/45-inch-wide lightweight woven fabric:
⅓ yard teal print
⅔ yard fusible web
9½ x 9½-inch square Timtex firm interfacing and stabilizer
Rayon embroidery thread
Yellow 6-strand embroidery floss
Buttons:
4 yellow ⅝-inch
4 green ⅜-inch
4 assorted glass beads

Cutting

From teal print:

• Cut two 10 x 10-inch squares.

From fusible web:

• Cut two 10 x 10-inch squares.

Assembly

Apply fusible web squares to wrong sides of fabric squares following manufacturer's instructions. Fuse bonded fabric squares to both sides of interfacing square.

Enlarge tea bag holder template (see page 86) 200 per cent. Trace enlarged template, including centre square, onto one side of assembled unit. *Note: Traced lines will be covered by stitching.* Cut out on outer traced lines.

Cover traced lines for centre square using a machine satin stitch (Figure 16).

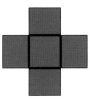

Figure 16

Satin-stitch around outer edge of tea bag holder, allowing needle on outside edge to fall off holder's edge.

Fold up sides of holder and tack in place with 6-strand embroidery floss, tying ends of floss through layered buttons. Attach beads to ends of floss at one corner. Trim ends of floss as desired on remaining corners. ■

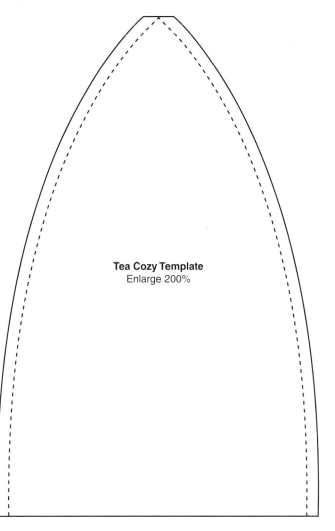

Tea Cozy Template
Enlarge 200%

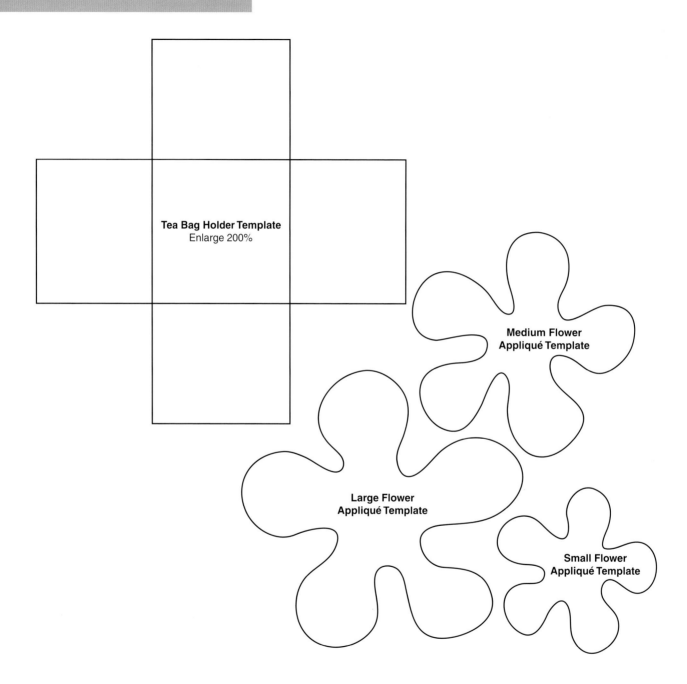

Tea Bag Holder Template
Enlarge 200%

**Medium Flower
Appliqué Template**

**Large Flower
Appliqué Template**

**Small Flower
Appliqué Template**

FLOWERS & STRIPES TABLECLOTH

Pick a floral home decor fabric and accent it with a strong stripe fabric to create this luxurious table topper. But keep your secret to yourself; there's no need to let anyone know you did this in a weekend.

Designs | Carol Zentgraf

Skill Level
Beginner

Finished Sizes
Tablecloth: 60 x 84 inches
Napkin: 20 x 20 inches
Napkin Ring: 2 inches wide x 2 inches in diameter

Materials for Tablecloth, & Four Napkins & Rings
44-inch-wide cotton fabric:
    3½ yards floral print
    2½ yards coordinating stripe
4 (1-inch-diameter) covered-button forms
18-inch ruler

Cutting
From floral print:
• Cut one 43 x 67-inch rectangle for tablecloth centre panel.

• Cut four 22 x 22-inch squares for napkins.

• Cut four scraps of fabric to cover buttons for napkin rings.

From coordinating stripe:
• Cut eight 10½-inch strips across the width of the fabric.

• Cut four 5 x 8-inch strips for napkin rings.

Assembly
Use ½-inch-wide seam allowances unless otherwise indicated. Sew right sides together.

Sew short edges of stripe strips together, matching stripes, to make four 88-inch strips. Press seam allowances open. Fold each stripe strip in half, using the centre seam as the guide. Cut two strips to 86 inches long and two to 62 inches long for border strips by removing length from outside strips.

Mark the centre of each side of the centre panel. Pin border strips to corresponding edges, matching centre marks to border centre seams. Sew border strips to centre panel, stitching to ½ inch from each corner.

To mitre border strips at each corner, fold the corner in half with right sides together and adjacent border strips even.

Pin the loose ends of the strips together. With 18-inch ruler aligned with the fold, draw a line from the end of the stitching to the corner of the border strips (Figure 1). Pin strips together along the line. Stitch along the line and trim excess corner fabric. Press seams open.

Figure 1

Press tablecloth edges under in a ½-inch double hem. Topstitch in place ⅜ inch from the outside edge.

On opposite edges of 22 x 22-inch square for napkin, press under a doubled ½-inch hem and topstitch. Repeat for remaining edges. Repeat for remaining napkins.

To make napkin ring, fold 5 x 8-inch stripe strip in half lengthwise with right sides together. Sew long edges and one short edge together. Trim seam allowance. Turn right side out and press. Press raw open edge under. Edgestitch around all edges.

Cover button with scrap of floral print fabric following manufacturer's instructions. Overlap ends of strip 1 inch. Sew button in place through strip ends to secure. Repeat for remaining napkin rings. ■

Flowers & Stripes Tablecloth

CAREFREE PICNIC SET

Fashion a waterproof oilcloth ground cover or tablecloth and accessories for a carefree picnic. The colourful oilcloth fabric makes cleanup a breeze.

Designs | Janis Bullis

Skill Level
Intermediate

Finished Sizes
Tablecloth: 40 x 40 inches
Placemat: 12 x 18 inches
Self-lined basket liner: 29 x 32 inches when flat; fits picnic basket 14½ x 10½ x 10½ inches

Materials
47-inch-wide oilcloth:
    3 yards main colour
    2 yards coordinating colour
Grosgrain ribbon:
    2 yards ⅜-inch-wide
    1 yard ⅝-inch-wide
All-purpose sewing thread
Air-soluble fabric marking pen
Craft paper

Tablecloth

Cutting
From main-colour oilcloth:
• Cut one 35 x 35-inch square for tablecloth centre.

• Cut one 42 x 42-inch square for lining.

From coordinating-colour oilcloth:
• Cut four contrasting borders each 3½ x 44 inches.

Assembly
Using air-soluble pen, on wrong side of fabric, mark a dot in each corner of the tablecloth centre ½ inch from each cut edge.

With right sides facing, the cut edges even, and with centres aligned, pin one long cut edge of one border to one edge of tablecloth body (see Pinning Tips on page 95). Stitch border to centre along one edge, using a ½-inch seam allowances, and beginning and ending with locked stitching at marked dots. Repeat for remaining three sides of centre with three remaining borders. Press seams open (see Pressing Tips on page 95).

To mark mitred-corner stitching line, fold the cloth in half diagonally with right sides facing and the cut edges of two adjacent borders even and aligned. Working on one corner at a time, push all seam allowances away from the border and toward the centre of the cloth. Using a straightedge, mark a line on the border fabric from the marked corner dot and in line with the fold of the tablecloth. Pin and stitch the borders together on the marked line beginning at the outer edge of the fabric and ending at the marked dot (Figure 1 page 92).

Carefree Picnic Set

Trim excess fabric to measure a ½-inch seam allowance and press seam open. Repeat for remaining three corners.

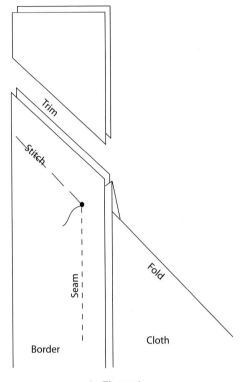

Figure 1

Position tablecloth top on tablecloth lining with right sides facing. Trim outside edges of lining to be even with outside edges of bordered cloth. Pin and stitch along all edges, leaving a large opening along one edge to turn. Press seams open and turn cloth through opening to the right side. Tuck in seam allowances along opening. Topstitching close to the folds, stitch open edge closed. Press cloth flat.

Placemat

Cutting for Each Placemat
From main-colour oilcloth:
• Cut one 10 x 16-inch rectangle for placemat centre.

• Cut one 14 x 20-inch rectangle for lining.

From coordinating-colour oilcloth:
• Cut two borders each 2½ x 16 inches.

• Cut 2 borders each 2½ x 22 inches.

Assembly
Follow tablecloth instructions substituting placemat centre and lining for tablecloth centre and lining. Align the short borders on the short sides of the placemat and long borders on the long sides.

Self-Lined Basket Cover

Pattern Preparation

Measure the inside width, depth and height of basket. Take a second, extended-height measurement by draping the tape measure about 3 inches over the top of the basket on the front edge.

Draw a paper pattern using these measurements as a guide and working with a series of rectangles (Figure 2). The pattern centre rectangle should measure the basket width by the basket depth. Each side section should measure height by depth. The forward and back section should measure width by extended height. Position these measured rectangles in a cross configuration as illustrated; add ½-inch seam allowances to all outside edges. Label this pattern piece "basket lining."

Using this pattern piece as a guide, trace another pattern piece and measure and trim 1½ inches from the forward and back section after the seam allowance has been added. Label this pattern piece "basket cover."

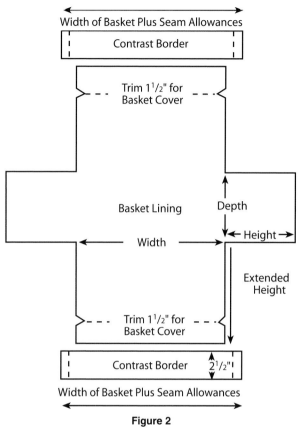

Figure 2

The third pattern piece is the contrast border. Cut it to measure 2½ inches tall x width of the front and back sections, including the seam allowances. Label this pattern piece "border."

Cutting
From main–colour oilcloth:
• Using the pattern pieces, cut one basket lining and one basket cover.

From coordinating–colour oilcloth:
• Using pattern piece, cut two borders.

From ⅝-inch-wide ribbon:
• Cut four ¼-yard lengths.

From ⅜-inch-wide ribbon:
• Cut eight ¼-yard lengths.

Assembly

With right sides facing, stitch each border to the front and back sections of the basket cover. Press seams open.

Fold each length of ⅝-inch-wide ribbon in half and pin the folded end to one end of each border. Measuring from the inside corners, pin one end of each ⅜-inch-wide ribbon length at seam line of each section (Figure 3). Use the basket height as your measurement.

With right sides together, pin assembled cover to the lining along all edges. Stitch edges of the cover, leaving an opening at one edge for turning and catching ribbon ends in stitching.

Turn assembly to right side; press flat. Tuck in seam allowances at opening edge and topstitch closed. Position basket cover inside basket and tie into place. ■

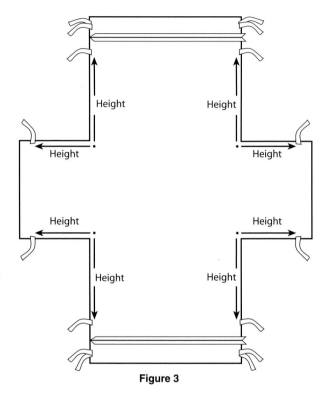

Figure 3

Working With Oilcloth

Cutting Tips

A pair of sharp, knife-edge shears will cut several layers of fabric easily. Rotary cutters will have no trouble, although it is recommended not to exceed two layers of fabric at a time because it tends to be of a slippery nature, and because of its density may walk across the table slightly under the push of a rotary cutter.

Pinning Tips

Do not pin in the body of your project. Once pin holes are formed, they can not be removed. Instead, position all pins within the seam allowances of the project—when positioning tissue pattern and when sewing seams.

Sewing Tips

Oilcloth can be sewn with little trouble on most sewing machines, providing they are in excellent operating condition with balanced tensions and include a new unused machine needle. Always test a scrap of fabric before sewing your project and follow these few tips for a carefree assembly.

When you are sewing seams with right sides of fabric together, consider increasing the stitch length slightly as the nature of this fabric has a tendency to drag a little. Always begin your project with a new all-purpose needle in an average size of 12/80. Use a high-quality, all-purpose sewing thread both in the needle and wound on the bobbin.

If topstitching proves to be difficult on your oilcloth project, it may be because the metal presser foot on your sewing machine is pulling against the vinyl. Many sewing machines have a plastic or nonstick-coated foot available as an accessory, designed just for this purpose. If a plastic foot is unavailable, consider using tissue paper strips while topstitching also. Cut wrapping paper tissue or an old tissue sewing pattern into narrow straight strips and place them under the presser foot. Sew through the tissue and both layers of fabric. Cut the strips narrow enough to keep the seam allowance gauge on the throat plate exposed.

If the right side of your fabric is facing against the feed-dog teeth, the teeth may have a tendency to scratch the vinyl. A layer of tissue paper may be necessary underneath the fabric also. Don't be afraid to work with tissue strips on top and bottom of the fabric if necessary.

Pressing Tips

Always use a warm (not hot) iron setting and a heavy, cotton press cloth when pressing oilcloth. Do not allow even a cool iron to directly touch the oilcloth on the right or wrong side.

SUSHI TIME PLACEMAT

Enjoy sushi and sauce with this fun twin-circular design to give each element its place.

Design | Linda Turner Griepentrog

Skill Level
Easy

Finished Size
19 x 12½ inches

Materials
⅜ yard 45-inch-wide oriental-print cotton fabric
1½ yards contrasting double-fold bias tape
Lightweight batting
2 inches ¼-inch-wide black elastic
Chinese coin and bead
Temporary spray adhesive

Cutting
From oriental print:
• Cut two 13 x 20-inch rectangles.

From batting:
• Cut one 13 x 20-inch rectangle.

Assembly
Using temporary spray adhesive, adhere the wrong side of each fabric rectangle to each side of batting rectangle.

Enlarge placemat pattern (see pages 98 & 99) 200 per cent. Trace pattern onto top fabric layer. Machine-stitch on traced line; trim close to stitching.

Bind raw edge with double-fold bias tape.

Make a small elastic loop; stitch ends together through the placemat at location indicated on pattern. Sew Chinese coin and bead over ends of elastic loop. ■

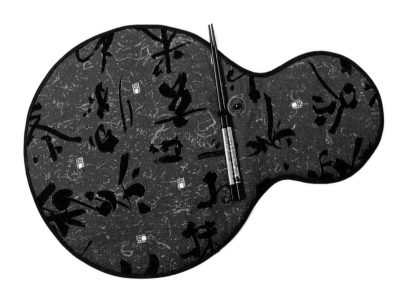

Sushi Time Placemat

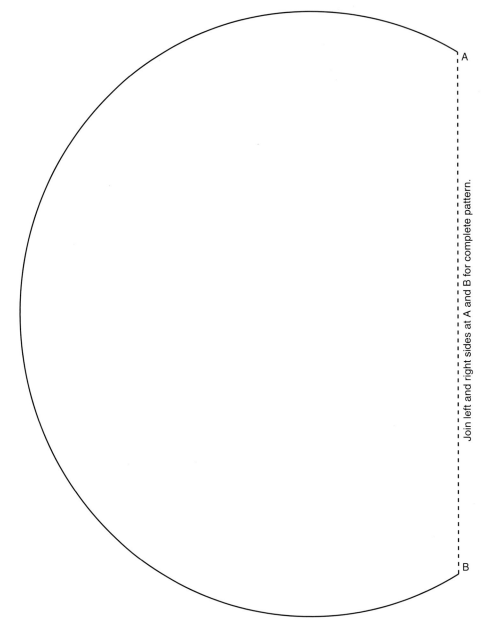

A

Join left and right sides at A and B for complete pattern.

B

Sushi Time Placemat (Left Side)
Enlarge Pattern 200%

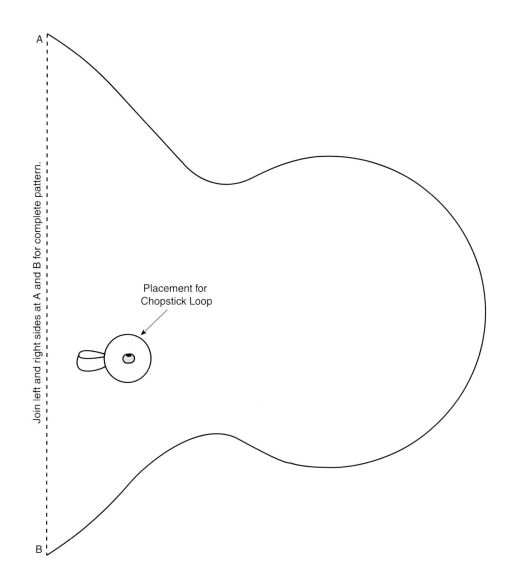

A

B

Join left and right sides at A and B for complete pattern.

Placement for
Chopstick Loop

Sushi Time Placemat (Right Side)
Enlarge Pattern 200%

SASSY SUNFLOWERS

Set a pretty fall table with this scalloped runner and matching placemats. Silk flowers make up the matching napkin rings.

Designs | Judith Sandstrom

Skill Level
Easy

Finished Sizes
Table Runner: 24 x 42 inches
Placemat: 12 x 18 inches
Napkin: 17½ x 17½ inches
Napkin Ring: 1¾ inches in diameter

Materials
Table Runner
44/45-inch-wide cotton fabrics:
- 1½ yards brown/off-white print for scallops and backing
- ½ yard off-white tone-on-tone print for runner centre
- ½ yard tone-on-tone yellow print for flowers
- ¼ yard green tone-on-tone print for leaves
- ⅛ yard brown tone-on-tone print for flower centres
- ⅛ yard green print for border

1 yard lightweight paper-backed fusible web tape
3¼ yards ¼-inch-wide iron-on fusible web
18 x 36-inch piece thin cotton batting
All-purpose thread to match appliqué fabrics

Two Placemats & Napkins
44/45-inch-wide cotton fabrics:
- ¾ yard brown/off-white print for scallops and backing
- ½ yard off-white tone-on-tone print for placemat centres

Two 8 x 14-inch pieces cotton batting
¼ yard or scraps of tone-on-tone prints in yellow, green and brown for appliqués
¾ yard green print for border and napkins
½ yard lightweight paper-backed fusible web
2½ yards ¼-inch-wide iron-on fusible web
All-purpose thread to match appliqué fabrics

Two Napkin Rings
2 silk sunflowers with a 6-inch wire stem
44/45-inch-wide cotton fabrics:
- 2 strips of brown/off-white print, each 1½ x 30 inches

Wire cutter

All Projects
Rotary cutter, mat and ruler
Template plastic
Pen or fine-tip marker
Small sharp scissors
Pinking shears

Note: Wash and iron all fabrics to remove wrinkles before cutting.

Sassy Sunflowers

Table Runner

Cutting

From off-white tone-on-tone print:
• Cut a rectangle 18 x 36 inches.

From yellow tone-on-tone print:
• On the paper side of a 17 x 18-inch piece of fusible web, trace eight sunflowers, using pattern on page 105. Leave ½ inch of space between the flowers. Apply the fusible web to the wrong side of the yellow tone-on-tone print. Cut out flowers along the traced lines and remove the backing paper.

From green tone-on-tone print:
• On the paper side of a 9 x 18-inch piece of fusible web, trace 16 leaves, using pattern on page 106. Leave ½ inch of space between the leaves. Apply the fusible web to the wrong side of the green tone-on-tone print. Cut out the leaves and remove the backing paper.

From brown tone-on-tone print:
• Trace eight sunflower centres, using pattern on page 105, onto a 4 x 17-inch strip of fusible web. Apply to the brown tone-on-tone print, cut out the sunflower centres and remove the backing paper.

From the green print for borders:
• Cut two strips each 1½ x 36 inches.

• Cut two strips each 1½ x 18½inches.

Assembly
Position the off-white tone-on-tone print rectangle on top of the batting rectangle and hand-baste the layers together ⅛ inch from the raw edges.

With right sides together, fold the piece of brown/off-white print in half so that it measures 27 x 43 inches.

With the off-white tone-on-tone print face up, centre the fabric/batting on the wrong side of the folded brown/off-white print fabric. Pin in place.

Trace the ½- and ¾-circle templates on page 106 onto template plastic and cut out. Place the ¾ circle at each corner of the off-white tone-on-tone print rectangle and trace around the outer edge to mark the scallops. Place the ½ circle next to the traced corner and trace around the curved outer edge. Move the ½ circle around the entire outer edge and trace around it to complete the scalloped edge (Figure 1). Unpin and remove the fabric/batting piece and set aside.

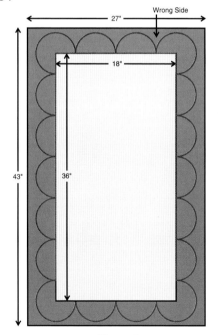

Figure 1

Pin the two layers of the brown print together. Stitch on the traced line. Using small sharp scissors, trim the seam allowance around each curve to ¼ inch. Clip the inner points to the stitching and use pinking shears to notch out the fullness around each curve.

Make a 6-inch-long slit in the centre of one of the two brown/off-white print fabric layers. Carefully turn the piece right side out through the slit and press carefully.

Arrange the sunflowers, centres and leaves around the perimeter of the off-white tone-on-tone print so they are at least 2 inches from the edges and about 5 inches apart. When pleased with the arrangement, fuse in place following the manufacturer's directions.

Using thread to match the appliqués and a short, narrow zigzag setting, stitch around the outer edge of each appliqué. Pull the threads to the back of the batting, knot and trim the ends. Begin with the leaves, and then do the flowers and the centres.

Machine-baste ½ inch from each raw edge of the layered runner and batting.

With right sides together, pin a 1½ x 36-inch green strip to each long edge of the runner centre with the raw edge along the basting. Stitch ¼ inch from the raw edges. Press the strip toward the seam allowance.

Sew the 1½ x 18½ -inch strips to the short ends of the runner in the same manner (Figure 2).

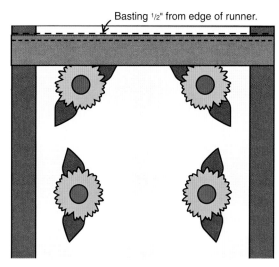

Basting ½" from edge of runner.

Figure 2

Following the manufacturer's directions, apply the ¼-inch-wide fusible web tape to the right side of each green border strip along the raw edges. Remove the backing paper.

Centre the runner on the scalloped border/backing unit, with the slit side against the batting. Turn under the raw edges of the border around the raw edges of the runner centre and finger-press. Check to make sure the runner is perfectly centred on the scalloped background before fusing the border edges in place.

Using green thread, stitch along the inner and outer edges of the green print to complete the table runner (see Figure 3 page 104).

Figure 3

Placemats & Napkins

Cutting

From yellow, green and brown tone-on-tone prints for appliqués:
• Using patterns on pages 105 and 106, trace four sunflower centres, four centres and eight leaves on the paper side of the fusible web, leaving space between the pieces and keeping the same shapes together in one area of the paper. Cut out the pieces in groups and apply each one to the wrong side of the appropriate scrap.
Cut out each shape and remove the backing paper.

From the green print:
• Cut two 18-inch squares for the napkins.

• Cut four strips each 1 x 14 inches.

• Cut four strips each 1 x 9 inches.

From the brown/off-white print:
• Cut four pieces each 12½ x 18½ inches.

From the off-white tone-on-tone print:
• Cut two pieces each 8 x 14 inches.

Assembly
With right sides facing, stitch the 12½ x 18½-inch brown/off-white print pieces together in pairs, stitching ¼ inch from the raw edges. Carefully make a 6-inch-long slit in one layer of each pair. Clip the corners and turn right side out through the slit. Press carefully.

With the off-white tone-on-tone print face up on the batting, machine-baste ¼ inch from the raw edges.

Position the sunflowers, leaves and sunflower centres on the off-white tone-on-tone print at opposite corners and at least ¾ inch from the raw edges. Fuse in place following manufacturer's directions. Using thread to match the appliqués and a short, narrow zigzag, stitch around the outer edge of each motif. Pull threads to the back of the batting, knot and trim ends.

With right sides together and raw edges even, pin a 1 x 14-inch green print strip to each long edge of the place-mat centre. Stitch ¼ inch from the raw edges. Press the strips toward the seam allowances. Add the 1 x 9-inch green print strips to the short ends in the same manner.

Following the manufacturer's directions, apply the ¼-inch-wide fusible web tape to the right side of each green border strip along the raw edges. Remove the backing paper. Turn under the raw edge and finger-press in place.

Centre the placemat centre on the slit side of the brown rectangle. When perfectly aligned, fuse in place.

Using green thread, stitch along the inner and outer edges of the green borders to complete the placemat.

Make narrow double hems along each edge of each napkin.

Napkin Ring

For each napkin ring, turn under and press ¼ inch along each raw edge of a 1½ x 30-inch brown/off-white print strip. Fold in half lengthwise with turned edges aligned and edgestitch to make a finished ½-inch-wide band.

If the silk sunflower has leaves, slide them up the stem so they are close to the flower.

Bend the wire stem into a 1¾-inch-diameter circle and twist the wire ends around themselves twice to secure. Trim off excess with the wire cutter.

Leaving a 6-inch-long section of the brown/off-white print band free and beginning at the underside of the flower, wind the band tightly around the curved stem, overlapping at ¼-inch intervals or less.

Tie the band ends together in a bow to complete the napkin ring. ∎

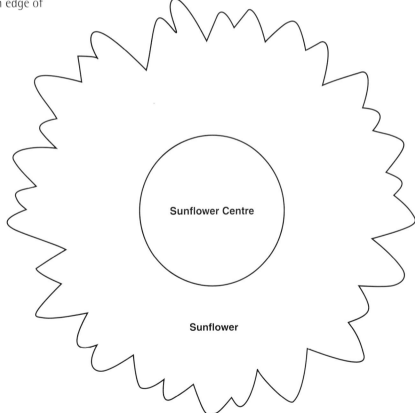

Sunflower Centre

Sunflower

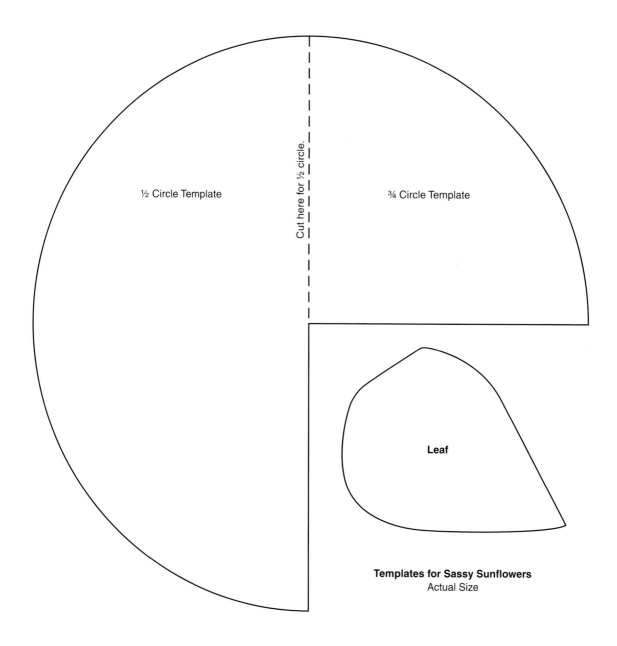

½ Circle Template

Cut here for ½ circle.

¾ Circle Template

Leaf

Templates for Sassy Sunflowers
Actual Size

In the Pumpkin Patch

Mix and match varying tone-on-tone prints and solids in autumn shades for a patch of colourful pumpkins to set your Halloween or Thanksgiving table.

Designs | Vandarra Robbins

Skill Level
Easy

Finished Sizes
Placemat: 13 x 14 inches
Table Runner: 60 inches long (adjust the length by adding or eliminating one or more pumpkins)

Materials for One Placemat
2 (10 x 12-inch) pieces orange print for pumpkin
2 (3-inch) squares green print for stem
2 (4 x 14-inch) pieces green print for leaves
1 (15-inch) square thin cotton batting
Rayon embroidery thread in green and brown
Tear-away or iron-away stabilizer
Temporary spray adhesive
Seam sealant
Sewing machine with zigzag feature

Materials for Each Pumpkin in Table Runner
2 (7 x 9-inch) pieces orange print for pumpkin
2 (3 x 3½-inch) green or tan print for stem
2 (3 x 10-inch) green print for leaves
11-inch square of thin batting
Rayon embroidery thread in green and brown
Tear-away or iron-away stabilizer
Temporary spray adhesive
Seam sealant
Sewing machine with zigzag feature

Notes: Use assorted printed cotton fabrics to make the pumpkins. Yardage given is for each pumpkin so you can customize the runner to suit your table length.

For the 60-inch length shown, you will need fabrics for eight different pumpkins in the amounts listed above. You can make each pumpkin from a different print or make more than one pumpkin from each of the prints.

Cutting for the Placemat
Enlarge the pumpkin pattern on page 111 by 200 per cent. Separate the stem and leaves from the pumpkin shape by cutting carefully along the lines. The pieces must fit back together again like a puzzle.

From orange print, green print for stem and green print for leaves:
• Fold each fabric in half with wrong sides together and use the pattern pieces to cut two each of the pumpkin, stem and leaves from the appropriate fabrics. Lightly trace the pumpkin section lines on the right side of one of the pumpkin pieces.

From the batting:
• Cut one each of the pumpkin, stem and leaves shapes.

Placemat Assembly

Apply a light coating of temporary spray adhesive to one side of the batting pumpkin. Smooth the marked pumpkin piece in place on top with raw edges matching. Trim batting even with pumpkin if necessary.

Turn the pumpkin over and add the remaining pumpkin layer in the same manner. Machine-baste ⅛ inch from the raw edges. Repeat to prepare the leaves and stem.

Adjust the machine for a narrow, closely spaced satin stitch and attach the appropriate presser foot. With brown embroidery thread in the needle, satin-stitch on the pumpkin section lines.

With a layer of stabilizer positioned underneath and extending beyond the upper edge of the pumpkin shape, butt the cut edge of the stem against the pumpkin cut edge.

Set the machine for a medium-width, medium-length zigzag stitch and stitch the pieces together. Adjust the machine for a medium-width satin stitch and thread the needle with green embroidery thread. Beginning in the centre of the zigzagged edge, satin-stitch over the zigzagging (Figure 1). Pivot and continue around the stem.

Note: Make sure that every outward swing of the needle pierces the stabilizer along the outer edges of the fabric shapes so that all raw edges are completely covered with satin stitches.

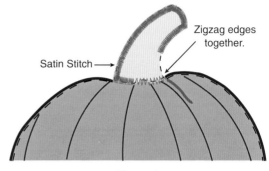

Figure 1
Satin-Stiching Stem

When you reach the beginning of the satin stitching, stop and pull threads to the underside to tie off. Apply seam sealant to the knots to secure them; allow to dry.

Add the leaves to the bottom edge of the pumpkin as described for the stem.

With brown embroidery thread, satin-stitch over the outer edges of the pumpkin. When you reach the stem or leaf stitching, backstitch a few stitches and then pull the threads to the underside to tie off. Treat the knots with seam sealant and allow to dry.

Remove the stabilizer following the manufacturer's directions. If fabric and backing extend beyond the outer edges of the satin stitching, trim carefully to avoid cutting the satin stitches.

In the Pumpkin Patch

Cutting for the Table Runner

Enlarge pumpkin pattern 150 per cent for the table runner.

From orange print, green or tan print for stem and green print for leaves:

• Cut the pieces for each of the eight pumpkins from the desired fabrics as directed for the placemat.

Table Runner Assembly

Follow the assembly directions for the placemat above to create eight pumpkins in assorted fabric combinations.

Alternating the stem placement from one side to the other (see photo page 109), arrange pumpkins as desired. Overlap pumpkins by ½ inch (more or less to adjust the finished length as desired). Use a bar tack or other decorative satin stitch of your choice to sew the two layers together (Figure 2). ■

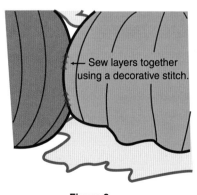

Sew layers together using a decorative stitch.

Figure 2

Satin Stitch Tapering

To satin-stitch smooth, ravel-free points, stitch toward the point and stop stitching when the width of the remaining point is the same width as the satin stitch. Continue stitching, stopping often to gradually decrease the stitch width so that the width is 0 when you reach the point. Leave the needle in the fabric and pivot. Continue stitching, gradually increasing the stitch width to match the original width. This technique prevents lumps and loose and unsightly satin stitches that hang off the points.

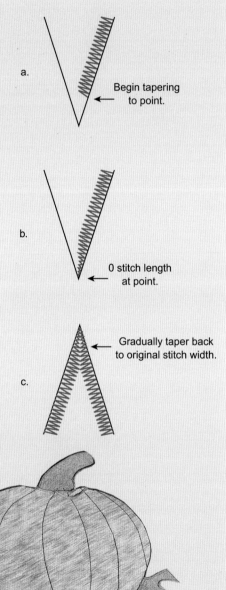

a. Begin tapering to point.

b. 0 stitch length at point.

c. Gradually taper back to original stitch width.

Pumpkin Template
Enlarge 150% for table runner.
Enlarge 200% for placemat.

BALI
TABLECLOTH

Capture the beautiful colours of falling leaves with a selection of batik fabrics. The appliquéd leaf shapes scattered around the table topper will dress up your autumn decor.

Design | Lucy A. Fazely & Michael L. Burns

Skill Level
Beginner

Finished Size
41 x 41 inches

Materials
44/45-inch-wide fabrics:
 1¼ yards cream batik
 8 fat eighths batik prints in fall colours
  for appliqués
Template plastic or thin, sturdy cardboard
1¼ yards 12-inch-wide fusible web
⅔ yard 20-inch-wide tear-away stabilizer

Tablecloth
Fold the 1¼-yard piece of cream batik in half lengthwise. Fold in half again crosswise (Figure 1).

Trim the folded fabric to measure 21 x 21 inches (Figure 2). Cut the excess from the selvage and raw edges only. Do not cut at the folded edges. *Note: If the fabric is not wide enough to trim to this size, trim to 20 x 20 inches instead.*

With the fabric square still folded, mark and cut away a 12¼-inch triangle at the corner with the cut edges (Figure 3). *Note: Cut away an 11¾-inch triangle if your trimmed square is only 20 x 20 inches.*

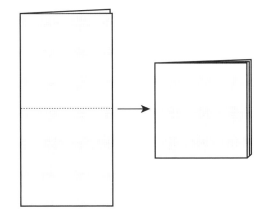

Figure 1

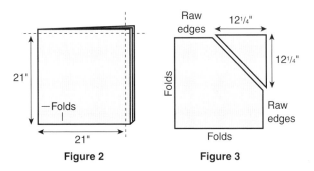

Figure 2   **Figure 3**

Turn under, press and stitch a narrow finished hem on all edges of tablecloth.

Bali Tablecloth

Fold the tablecloth into eighths and press to mark the sections. Open the tablecloth (Figure 4).

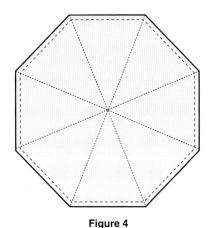

Figure 4

Leaf Appliqués

On the paper side of the fusible web, trace around the leaf template 16 times. Leave ½ inch of space between shapes. Reverse the template and trace 16 more leaves (32 leaves total).

Cut out the leaves in groups of four. Remove the backing paper and fuse the groups on the wrong sides of the appliqué fabrics. Cut out each leaf on the traced lines.

Referring to the photo (see page 113), arrange the leaves in four alternating sections of the tablecloth. Place five leaves above the hemmed edge in each section and three falling leaves in the area above each five-leaf group. Pin each leaf in place.

Lightly fuse the leaves in place. Remove pins and cover leaves with a press cloth to protect the iron. Fuse leaves permanently in place following the manufacturer's directions.

Position a piece of tear-away stabilizer under each leaf on the wrong side of the tablecloth and pin in place.

Set the machine for a short, narrow zigzag stitch. Machine-appliqué each leaf in place. Use the same stitch setting to embroider the stem/vein on each leaf. For emphasis, zigzag again over the first stem/vein stitching in each leaf. Remove the tear-away stabilizer. ■

Leaf Template

PUMPKIN TABLE SETTING

Add pumpkin appliqués to a purchased placemat, matching napkins and a bread-basket cover to set a festive fall table.

Designs | Angie Wilhite

Skill Level
Beginner

Finished Sizes
Finished sizes of purchased items may vary.

Materials For One Table Setting & Bread-Basket Cover
12 x 18-inch purchased natural placemat
12-inch-square purchased natural luncheon napkin
18-inch-square purchased natural dinner
    napkin for bread-basket cover
44/45-inch-wide fabrics for appliqués:
    ¼ yard orange check for
        pumpkins
    ⅙ yard tan for stems
    ⅙ yard green for leaves
All-purpose thread to match fabrics
Rayon embroidery thread to match
    appliqué fabrics
¼ yard fusible web
¼ yard tear-away stabilizer
⅛ yard fusible interfacing

Preparation & Assembly
Prewash the purchased placemat and
napkins and the appliqué fabrics.

Do not use fabric softener in the washer or dryer. Press to remove all wrinkles.

Enlarge the pumpkin pattern (see page 116) 200 per cent for the placemat.

On the paper side of the fusible web, trace five small pumpkins and one large pumpkin, leaving ½ inch of space between each shape. Trace one large and five small stems, and one large and five small leaves. Cut out each shape, leaving a ¼-inch margin beyond the traced lines (Figure 1).

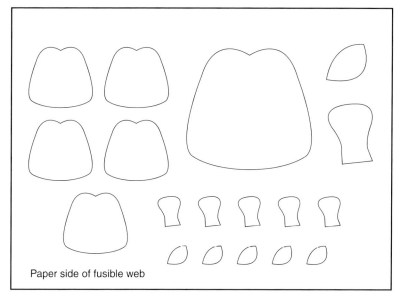

Paper side of fusible web

Figure 1

Apply fusible interfacing to the wrong side of the green fabric for the leaves for added stability.

Position the large and small pumpkin shapes on the wrong side of the orange check fabric and lightly fuse in place. Allow to cool. Cut out each shape on the traced lines. Repeat this process with the stems on the tan fabric, and the leaves on the interfaced green fabric to prepare all remaining appliqués (Figure 2).

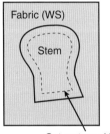

Cut on traced line.

Figure 2

Remove the paper backing from the large pumpkin and stem shapes. Position the pumpkin in the lower left corner of the placemat and tuck the stem underneath. Fuse the pieces in place following the manufacturer's directions.

Position and fuse the stems and pumpkins in the corners of the large napkin and in one corner of the small napkin.

Pin or baste tear-away stabilizer on the wrong side of the placemat and napkins under each appliqué.

Adjust the machine for a closely spaced, medium-width satin stitch. With rayon embroidery thread on the top and all-purpose thread in the bobbin, satin-stitch around the stems and then the pumpkin on each piece.

Remove the paper backing from the leaves. Position a leaf on each pumpkin and fuse in place. Satin-stitch around each leaf, beginning and ending at a point on each one. Remove the stabilizer and trim the threads. ■

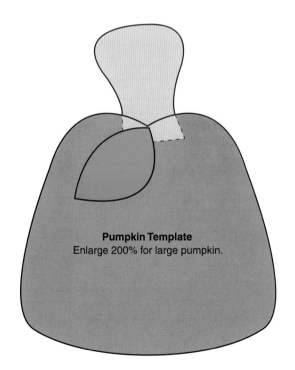

Pumpkin Template
Enlarge 200% for large pumpkin.

Pumpkin Table Setting

FALLING LEAVES LUNCHEON SET

Colourful fall foliage frames the borders of this simply styled placemat. Matching napkins add a finishing touch to the table.

Designs | Marta Alto

Skill Level
Easy

Finished Sizes
Placemat: 12 x 18 inches
Napkin: 18 x 18 inches

Materials for Four Place Settings
44/45-inch-wide cotton fabric:
⅞ yard brown tone-on-tone print for borders
2½ yards rust solid or tone-on-tone print for placemat centres and backings, and napkins
1 yard 45-inch-wide polyester fleece
¼-inch-wide fusible web
Leaf embroidery design of your choice
Polyester or rayon embroidery thread in fall colours for leaves
Water-soluble liquid stabilizer
Sewing machine with computerized embroidery unit and hoop
Serger

Cutting
Preshrink the fabrics before cutting the pieces.

From rust solid or print for placemat centres and napkins:
• Cut four 18-inch squares for the napkins.

• Cut four 6½ x 12½-inch rectangles for centres.

• Cut four 12½ x 18½-inch rectangles for backings.

From brown print for borders:
• Cut six 4½ x 40-inch strips; subcut strips into eight each 4½ x 6½-inch and 4½ x 20½-inch strips for borders.
Note: These strips are cut wider than necessary; you will trim them to size after embroidering the assembled placemat panels.

From polyester fleece:
• Cut four 12½ x 18½-inch rectangles.

Placemat Assembly
Use ¼-inch seam allowances unless otherwise indicated.

Sew a short border strip to each short edge of each placemat centre. Press.

Add a long border strip to the top and bottom edges of each placemat centre (Figure 1). Press.

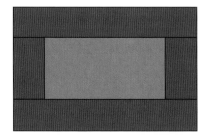

Figure 1

Falling Leaves Luncheon Set

Apply liquid stabilizer to each placemat front and allow to dry. Apply stabilizer to one corner of each napkin square in an area that measures approximately 6 inches square. Allow to dry. Press.

Load the embroidery design into the embroidery unit. Two sets of leaves are required at the long seam lines and only one set at the short seam lines. Choose several different leaf embroideries and combine them to make your own design for the placemats and napkins.

Mark the centres for each leaf design at each placemat seam line, remembering to mirror-image the designs for the opposite borders.

Complete the embroideries on each placemat and remove the stabilizer following the package directions. Dry and press.

Trim border on each placemat to 3¼ inches wide.

Apply a light coat of temporary spray adhesive to one side of each fleece rectangle and smooth in place on the wrong side of a backing rectangle.

With right sides together, stitch each placemat to a fleece-backed rectangle, leaving a 5-inch opening in one long edge for turning (Figure 2). Clip the corners to eliminate bulk and turn the placemat right side out through the opening. Gently shape each corner. Press outer edges so the backing doesn't show.

Fuse the opening edges together with a strip of fusible web.

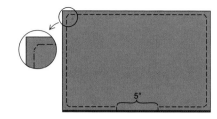

Figure 2

Napkin Assembly

Mark the embroidery placement in the corner of each napkin square. Baste scrap strips of fabric to the adjacent corners of each napkin square as shown in Figure 3 to make it possible to hoop the fabric for embroidery. Fold each prepared napkin in half diagonally to mark the centreline. Hoop the napkin corner diagonally to complete the embroidery. Do not remove the stabilizer yet.

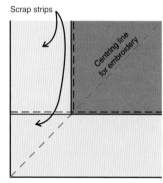

Figure 3

Thread the serger with serger thread in the needle and lower looper, and topstitching thread in the upper looper. Adjust the serger for a rolled-edge stitch and test on a fabric scrap. Finish the raw edges of each napkin. *Note: If you prefer, make a double narrow hem at the napkin edges.*

Wash the napkins to remove the stabilizer; press. ■

Handwoven Textile Mats

Unique handwoven textiles are the main attraction when used to create easy-to-sew placemats and napkins.

Designs | Lisa Shepard

Self-Fringed Placemat & Napkins

Skill Level
Beginner

Finished Sizes
Adjustable

Materials for Two Place Settings
1 yard 18–19-inch-wide handwoven fabric*
½ yard of coordinating handwoven fabric for napkins**
Masking tape
Fusible tape (optional)
Sewing thread to match fabrics

* If handwoven fabric is wider than 19 inches, cut it to 20 inches and hem 1 inch on each side.

**Depending on the weight and washability of the placemat fabric, you can cut matching napkins from the same fabric or select a coordinating machine-washable cotton or linen fabric instead.

Placemat
Note: Instructions are given for making single placemat.

The width of the placemat is determined by the width of the handwoven fabric. Decide on the desired top-to-bottom measurement for placemat; add length needed for the fringe that will extend off edge of the table; add 1 inch for top hem allowance. This is the cutting measurement (for example, a 13-inch placemat, plus a 2-inch fringe, plus a 1-inch hem allowance for the top edge totals 16 inches of fabric length needed).

Mark a cutting line for fabric length on right side of fabric. On wrong side of fabric, place masking tape centred over cutting lines (masking tape will prevent the fabric from raveling when cut). Cut taped fabric into sections.

Turn 1 inch under at top edge of each fabric piece and hem by machine, by hand or with fusible tape.

Measure from bottom edge the number of inches allowed for fringe and straight-stitch along fabric piece at this point. Remove the horizontal, or weft, threads from fabric piece, using a pin to loosen them and pulling no more than two to three strands at a time. The remaining vertical threads, or warp fibres, will become the fringe.

Taking a few strands at a time, twist the warp fibres into fringe by rolling the yarns between your fingers, or using a two-strand twist. *Note: If desired, beads may be added at different midpoints along each fringe.* Work across the width of the placemat.

Stitch another line of straight stitching ½ inch below the first, to secure fringe.

Napkins
For each napkin, cut one 14- to 16-inch square from fabric. Hem raw edges as desired or stitch and fringe the edges same as for the placemat.

Placemats With Easy-Finish Piping

Finished Sizes
Adjustable

Materials for Two Place Settings
1 yard 18–19-inch-wide handwoven fabric*
½ yard coordinating handwoven fabric for napkins**
4 yards coordinating piping
Masking tape
Fusible tape (optional)
Sewing thread to match fabrics

* If handwoven fabric is wider than 19 inches, cut it to 20 inches and hem 1 inch on each side.

**Depending on the weight and washability of the placemat fabric, you can cut matching napkins from the same fabric or select a coordinating machine-washable cotton or linen fabric instead.

Placemat
Note: Follow instructions for each placemat.

Determine desired size and shape of placemat. *Note: Consider oval, rounded, blunt-cut-corners or other shapes (Figure 1).* Add a seam allowance of ¾ inch all around.

OVAL   ROUNDED   BLUNT-CUT

Figure 1

Before cutting, mark cutting lines on right side of fabric; then centre masking tape over lines on wrong side of fabric to help prevent fraying and shifting of the weave as you cut. *Note: The tape may be left on the placemat to stabilize the seam allowance until the piping is stitched on, as long as the tape itself is not stitched through.*

Turn raw edge under ½ inch on all sides, or ¾ inch if fabric is bulky. Press. With right side of placemat facing up, position header of piping under folded edge and piping butted against edge of the placemat. Pin or baste in place. Topstitch close to edge of placemat. Where the ends of the piping meet, bring each end down under the placemat and overlap. Secure piping ends with a few hand stitches through the overlapped ends on wrong side.

Napkins
For each napkin, cut one 14- to 16-inch square from fabric. Hem raw edges as desired. ■

Handwoven Textile Mats

INDEX

INDEX

METRIC CONVERSION CHARTS

Metric Conversions

yards	x	.9144	=	metres (m)
yards	x	91.44	=	centimetres (cm)
inches	x	2.54	=	centimetres (cm)
inches	x	25.40	=	millimetres (mm)
inches	x	.0254	=	metres (m)

centimetres	x	.3937	=	inches
metres	x	1.0936	=	yards

Standard Equivalents

⅛ inch	=	3.20 mm	=	0.32 cm
¼ inch	=	6.35 mm	=	0.635 cm
⅜ inch	=	9.50 mm	=	0.95 cm
½ inch	=	12.70 mm	=	1.27 cm
⅝ inch	=	15.90 mm	=	1.59 cm
¾ inch	=	19.10 mm	=	1.91 cm
⅞ inch	=	22.20 mm	=	2.22 cm
1 inch	=	25.40 mm	=	2.54 cm
⅛ yard	=	11.43 cm	=	0.11 m
¼ yard	=	22.86 cm	=	0.23 m
⅜ yard	=	34.29 cm	=	0.34 m
½ yard	=	45.72 cm	=	0.46 m
⅝ yard	=	57.15 cm	=	0.57 m
¾ yard	=	68.58 cm	=	0.69 m
⅞ yard	=	80.00 cm	=	0.80 m
1 yard	=	91.44 cm	=	0.91 m

1⅛ yard	=	102.87 cm	=	1.03 m
1¼ yard	=	114.30 cm	=	1.14 m
1⅜ yard	=	125.73 cm	=	1.26 m
1½ yard	=	137.16 cm	=	1.37 m
1⅝ yard	=	148.59 cm	=	1.49 m
1¾ yard	=	160.02 cm	=	1.60 m
1⅞ yard	=	171.44 cm	=	1.71 m
2 yards	=	182.88 cm	=	1.83 m
2⅛ yards	=	194.31 cm	=	1.94 m
2¼ yards	=	205.74 cm	=	2.06 m
2⅜ yards	=	217.17 cm	=	2.17 m
2½ yards	=	228.60 cm	=	2.29 m
2⅝ yards	=	240.03 cm	=	2.40 m
2¾ yards	=	251.46 cm	=	2.51 m
2⅞ yards	=	262.88 cm	=	2.63 m
3 yards	=	274.32 cm	=	2.74 m
3⅛ yards	=	285.75 cm	=	2.86 m
3¼ yards	=	297.18 cm	=	2.97 m
3⅜ yards	=	308.61 cm	=	3.09 m
3½ yards	=	320.04 cm	=	3.20 m
3⅝ yards	=	331.47 cm	=	3.31 m
3¾ yards	=	342.90 cm	=	3.43 m
3⅞ yards	=	354.32 cm	=	3.54 m
4 yards	=	365.76 cm	=	3.66 m
4⅛ yards	=	377.19 cm	=	3.77 m
4¼ yards	=	388.62 cm	=	3.89 m
4⅜ yards	=	400.05 cm	=	4.00 m
4½ yards	=	411.48 cm	=	4.11 m
4⅝ yards	=	422.91 cm	=	4.23 m
4¾ yards	=	434.34 cm	=	4.34 m
4⅞ yards	=	445.76 cm	=	4.46 m
5 yards	=	457.20 cm	=	4.57 m